Beautiful Words by Beautiful People

What's a Song If It Can't Be Sung "1001 Quotations"

Cristina Eileen O'Connell

ISBN-13: **978-1537209555**
ISBN-10: **1537209558**

DEDICATION

I am very proud and excited to dedicate this special little book to my dear inspirational beautiful family, Mother Stephanie, Father Joe and brother Garreth O'Connell. I thank you for supporting me and inspiring me in all that I do. I am so humble and very grateful for your continued love and support.

Cristina Eileen O'Connell

Contents

"It's the simple things in life that bring the greatest joy" – Cristina Eileen O'Connell

Message from Cristina,

I am proud to present this book to all the beautiful people in this world. I hope you find peace and overwhelming joy within you.

My advice in reading this book is simply read the inspirational quotes and you alone can make sense of which individual quote can mean to you. You will discover how powerful a quote can affect your mood, your relationships and many other aspects of life.

I recommend when reading these powerful quotes from beautiful people, follow the steps provided below:

- Start with at least 5 quotes per day
- In your mind choose left or right page
- Pick a number between 1-5
- Flip through the book and stop where you feel you're guided to do so.
- Pick the quote in accordance to step 2 and 3

I promise you will find the understanding and knowledge of that quote. It will mean a lot to you on that day. Keep it up and it will manifest positive thoughts and feelings of abundance and love. The power is within you. Life is a gift and we are a gift to life. Know that you are unique and perfect exactly the way you are.

Life is wonderful. It is full of love, joy and happiness it is simply a matter of choice. Live the life you seek, live in the present moment, and know that tomorrow will take care of itself. A simple positive repetitive thought will guide you to feel peaceful, joyous, loved and fulfilled. Life is what you make it, so reach for the stars the sky's the limit, laugh often, spend time with love ones, take control of your actions anything is possible.

I hope you enjoy this book as much as I have enjoyed creating it for you. My wish is that it will bring more knowledge, awareness, prosperity, joy and harmony.

From my heart I love you all and thank you for allowing me to be a participant on your journey.

Love yourself and keep showing your beautiful smile to the world.

Lots of love, always your friend,

Cristina xxx

ACCEPTANCE

1. "When you find peace within yourself, you become the kind of person who can live at peace with others." - Peace Pilgrim

2. "Many of us crucify ourselves between two thieves - regret for the past and fear of the future." - Fulton Oursler

3. "Being happy doesn't mean that everything is perfect. It means that you've decided to look beyond the imperfections." - unknown

4. "As you become more clear about who you really are, you'll be better able to decide what is best for you - the first time around." - Oprah Winfrey

5. "Deep down even the most hardened criminal is starving for the same thing that motivates the innocent baby: Love and acceptance" - Lily Fairchilde

6. "A true man never frets about his place in the world, but just slides into it by the gravitation of his nature, and swings there as easily as a star." - Edwin Hubbel Chapin

7. "Some people confuse acceptance with apathy, but there's all the difference in the world. Apathy fails to distinguish between what can and what cannot be helped; acceptance makes that distinction. Apathy paralyzes the will-to-action; acceptance frees it by relieving it of impossible burdens." - Arthur Gordon

8. "The art of acceptance is the art of making someone who has just done you a small favor wish that he might have done you a greater one." - Martin Luther King, Jr.

9. "That is the definition of faith -- acceptance of that which we imagine to be true, that which we cannot prove." - Dan Brown

10. "California sunlight - sweet Calcutta rain - Honolulu starbright - the song remains the same." - Led Zeppelin

11. "But there isn't any second half of myself waiting to plug in and make me whole. It's there. I'm already whole." - Sally Field

12. "Acceptance is not submission; it is acknowledgement of the facts of a situation. Then deciding what you're going to do about it." - Kathleen Casey Theisen

13. "If a ship has been sunk, I can't bring it up. If it is going to be sunk, I can't stop it. I can use my time much better working on tomorrow's problem than by fretting about yesterday's. Besides, if I let those things get me, I wouldn't last long." - Admiral Ernest J. King

14. "The only thing that will make you happy is being happy with who you are, and not who people think you are." - Goldie Hawn

15. "Acceptance and tolerance and forgiveness, those are life-altering lessons." - Jessica Lange

16. "Acceptance is not love. You love a person because he or she has lovable traits, but you accept everybody just because they're alive and human." - Albert Ellis

17. "Acceptance of one's life has nothing to do with resignation; it does not mean running away from the struggle. On the contrary, it means accepting it as it comes, with all the handicaps of heredity, of suffering, of psychological complexes and injustices." - Paul Tournier

18. "Acceptance of what has happened is the first step to overcoming the consequences of any misfortune." - William James

19. "At the heart of personality is the need to feel a sense of being lovable without having to qualify for that acceptance." - Paul Tournier

20. "Happiness can exist only in acceptance." - George Orwell

21. "The first step toward change is awareness. The second step is acceptance." - Nathaniel Branden

22. "The greatest gift that you can give to others is the gift of unconditional love and acceptance." - Brian Tracy

23. "The keys to patience are acceptance and faith. Accept things as they are, and look realistically at the world around you. Have faith in yourself and in the direction you have chosen." - Ralph Marston

ACHIEVEMENT

24. " When we think of failure; Failure will be ours. If we remain undecided; nothing will ever change. All we need to do is want to achieve something great and then simply to do it. Never think of failure for what we think, will come about." -   Maharishi Mahesh Yogi

25. " The results you achieve will be in direct proportion to the effort you apply." -   Denis Waitley

26. " The truth of the matter is that there's nothing you can't accomplish if: (1) You clearly decide what it is that you're absolutely committed to achieving, (2) You're willing to take massive action, (3) You notice what's working or not, and (4) You continue to change your approach until you achieve what you want, using whatever life gives you along the way." -   Anthony Robbins

27. " That some achieve great success is proof to all that others can achieve it as well." -   Abraham Lincoln

28. " Build this day on a foundation of pleasant thoughts. Never fret at any imperfections that you fear may impede your progress. Remind yourself, as often as necessary, that you are a creature of God and have the power to achieve any dream by lifting up your thoughts. You can fly when you decide that you can. Never consider yourself defeated again. Let the vision in your heart be in your life's blueprint. Smile!"
-    Og Mandino

29. " Goals are a means to an end, not the ultimate purpose of our lives. They are simply a tool to concentrate our focus and move us in a direction. The only reason we really pursue goals is to cause ourselves to expand and grow. Achieving goals by themselves will never make us happy in the long term; it's who you become, as you overcome the obstacles necessary to achieve your goals, that can give you the deepest and most long-lasting sense of fulfillment." - Anthony Robbins

30. " The more you seek security, the less of it you have. But the more you seek opportunity, the more likely it is that you will achieve the security that you desire." - Brian Tracy

31. " When your desires are strong enough, you will appear to possess superhuman powers to achieve" -   Napoleon Hill

32. " All that a man achieves and all that he fails to achieve is the direct result of his own thoughts" -   James Allen

33. " You never achieve success unless you like what you are doing." -   Dale Carnegie

34. " Those who dare to fail miserably can achieve greatly." - John Fitzgerald Kennedy

35. " What we achieve inwardly will change outer reality." -   Plutarch

36. " No one lives long enough to learn everything they need to learn starting from scratch. To be successful, we absolutely, positively have to find people who have already paid the price to learn the things that we need to learn to achieve our goals." - Brian Tracy

37. " You have all the reason in the world to achieve your grandest dreams. Imagination plus innovation equals realization." -   Denis Waitley

38. " With our eyes fixed on the future, but recognizing the realities of today, we will achieve our destiny to be as a shining city on a hill for all mankind to see." -   Ronald Reagan

39. " Think of yourself as on the threshold of unparalleled success. A whole, clear, glorious life lies before you. Achieve! Achieve!" - Andrew Carnegie

40. " One must marry one's feelings to one's beliefs and ideas. That is probably the only way to achieve a measure of harmony in one's life." -   Napoleon Hill

41. " You cannot expect to achieve new goals or move beyond your present circumstances unless you change." -   Les Brown

42. " The person determined to achieve maximum success learns the principle that progress is made one step at a time. A house is built one brick at a time. Football games are won a play at a time. A department store grows bigger one customer at a time. Every big accomplishment is a series of little accomplishments." -   David Joseph Schwartz

43. " The three great essentials to achieve anything worthwhile are, first, hard work; second, stick-to-itiveness; third, common sense." -   Thomas Alva Edison

44. " Nothing average ever stood as a monument to progress. When progress is looking for a partner it doesn't turn to those who believe they are only average. It turns instead to those who are forever searching and striving to become the best they possibly can. If we seek the average level we cannot hope to achieve a high level of success. Our only hope is to avoid being a failure." -   A. Lou Vickery

45. " Be not afraid of greatness; some are born great, some achieve greatness, and others have greatness thrust upon them." - William Shakespeare

46. " Determine what specific goal you want to achieve. Then dedicate yourself to its attainment with unswerving singleness of purpose, the trenchant zeal of a crusader." - Paul J. Meyer

47. " You will achieve grand dream, a day at a time, so set goals for each day / not long and difficult projects, but chores that will take you, step by step, toward your rainbow. Write them down, if you must, but limit your list so that you won't have to drag today's undone matters into tomorrow. Remember that you cannot build your pyramid in twenty-four hours. Be patient. Never allow your day to become so cluttered that you neglect your most important goal / to do the best you can, enjoy this day, and rest satisfied with what you have accomplished."
-   Og Mandino

48. " We are built to conquer environment, solve problems, achieve goals, and we find no real satisfaction or happiness in life without obstacles to conquer and goals to achieve." -   Maxwell Maltz

49. " A person should set his goals as early as he can and devote all his energy and talent to getting there. With enough effort, he may achieve it. Or he may find something that is even more rewarding. But in the end, no matter what the outcome, he will know he has been alive." -   Walt Disney

50. " The person with a fixed goal, a clear picture of his desire, or an ideal always before him, causes it, through repetition, to be buried deeply in his subconscious mind and is thus enabled, thanks to its generative and sustaining power, to realize his goal in a minimum of time and with a minimum of physical effort. Just pursue the thought unceasingly. Step by step you will achieve realization, for all your faculties and powers become directed to that end." -   Claude M. Bristol

51. " If you wish to achieve worthwhile things in your personal and career life, you must become a worthwhile person in your own self-development." -   Brian Tracy

52. " To focus on technique is like cramming your way through school. You sometimes get by, perhaps even get good grades, but if you don't pay the price day in and day out, you'll never achieve true mastery of the subjects you study or develop an educated mind." - Stephen R. Covey

53. " If you can imagine it, you can achieve it; if you can dream it, you can become it." - William Arthur Ward

54. " What a great discrepancy there is between men and the results they achieve! It is due to the difference in their power of calling together all the rays of their ability, and concentrating them upon one point" - Orison Swett Marden

55. " Nothing stops the man who desires to achieve. Every obstacle is simply a course to develop his achievement muscle. It's a strengthening of his powers of accomplishment." -   Eric Butterworth

56. " Not the maker of plans and promises, but rather the one who offers faithful service in small matters. This is the person who is most likely to achieve what is good and lasting." -   Johann Wolfgang von Goethe

57. " To desire is to obtain; to aspire is to achieve." -   James Allen

ACTION

58. "Whatever course you decide upon, there is always someone to tell you that you are wrong. There are always difficulties arising which tempt you to believe that your critics are right. To map out a course of action and follow it to an end requires courage." -   Ralph Waldo Emerson

59. "It is not the critic who counts; not the man who points out how the strong man stumbles, or where the doer of deeds could have done them better. The credit belongs to the man who is actually in the arena, whose face is marred by dust and sweat and blood, who strives valiantly; who errs and comes short again and again; because there is not effort without error and shortcomings; but who does actually strive to do the deed; who knows the great enthusiasm, the great devotion, who spends himself in a worthy cause, who at the best knows in the end the triumph of high achievement and who at the worst, if he fails, at least he fails while daring greatly. So that his place shall never be with those cold and timid souls who know neither victory nor defeat." -   Theodore Roosevelt

60. " Knowing is not enough; we must apply. Willing is not enough; we must do." - Johann Wolfgang von Goethe

61. " Thinking is easy, acting is difficult, and to put one's thoughts into action is the most difficult thing in the world." -   Johann Wolfgang von Goethe

62. " I have been impressed with the urgency of doing. Knowing is not enough; we must apply. Being willing is not enough; we must do." -   Leonardo da Vinci

63. " Don't wait. The time will never be just right." -   Napoleon Hill

64. " When I stand before God at the end of my life, I would hope that I would not have a single bit of talent left, and could say, "I used everything you gave me." -   Erma Bombeck

65. " The more you are willing to accept responsibility for your actions, the more credibility you will have" -   Brian Koslow

66. " I never worry about action, but only about inaction" -   Winston Churchill

67. " Believe and act as if it were impossible to fail." -   Charles F. Kettering

68. " Everything you want is out there waiting for you to ask. Everything you want also wants you. But you have to take action to get it." -   Jules Renard

69. " Action is the real measure of intelligence." -   Napoleon Hill

70. " The possibilities are numerous once we decide to act and not react." -   George Bernard Shaw

71. " It is not only what we do, but also what we do not do, for which we are accountable." -   Moliere

72. " The ancestor of every action is a thought." -   Ralph Waldo Emerson

73. " To map out a course of action and follow it to an end requires courage" - Ralph Waldo Emerson

74. " Great acts are made up of small deeds." -   Lao Tzu

75. " The path to success is to take massive, determined action." -   Anthony Robbins

76. " Beings are owners of their action, heirs of their action." -   Buddha

77. " You see, in life, lots of people know what to do, but few people actually do what they know. Knowing is not enough! You must take action." -   Anthony Robbins

78. " Motivation is what gets you started. Habit is what keeps you going." -   Jim Rohn

79. " Risk! Risk anything! Care no more for the opinions of others, for those voices. Do the hardest thing on earth for you. Act for yourself. Face the truth." -   Katherine Mansfield

80. " When it is obvious that the goals cannot be reached, don't adjust the goals, adjust the action steps." -   Confucius

81. " Whatever you do may seem insignificant, but it is most important that you do it" -   Mahatma Gandhi

82. " You may never know what results come of your action, but if you do nothing there will be no result" -   Mahatma Gandhi

83. " Often the difference between a successful person and a failure is not one has better abilities or ideas, but the courage that one has to bet on one's ideas, to take a calculated risk - and to act." -   Andre Malraux

84. " The only cure for grief is action." -   G. H. Lewes

85. " Success seems to be connected with action. Successful people keep moving. They make mistakes, but they don't quit." - Conrad Hilton

86. " Behave so the aroma of your actions may enhance the general sweetness of the atmosphere." -   Henry David Thoreau

87. " We become just by performing just actions, temperate by performing temperate actions, brave by performing brave actions." -   Aristotle

88. " Dreams pass into the reality of action. From the actions stems the dream again; and this interdependence produces the highest form of living." -   Anais Nin

89. " Words may show a man's wit, but actions his meaning" -   Benjamin Franklin

90. " Inaction breeds doubt and fear. Action breeds confidence and courage. If you want to conquer fear, do not sit home and think about it. Go out and get busy." -   Dale Carnegie

91. " As you begin changing your thinking, start immediately to change your behaviour. Begin to act the part of the person you would like to become. Take action on your behaviour. Too many people want to feel, then take action. This never works." - John Maxwell

92. " Action may not bring happiness but there is no happiness without action." - William James

93. " Thoughts lead on to purpose, purpose leads on to actions, actions form habits, habits decide character, and character fixes our destiny" -   Tryon Edwards

94. "It's the little things you do that can make a big difference. What are you attempting to accomplish? What little thing can you do today that will make you more effective? You are probably only one step away from greatness." - Bob Proctor

95. " High achievers spot rich opportunities swiftly, make big decisions quickly and move into action immediately. Follow these principles and you can make your dreams come true." -   Robert H. Schuller

ATTITUDE

96. "Seek out that particular mental attribute which makes you feel most deeply and vitally alive, along with which comes the inner voice which says, 'This is the real me,' and when you have found that attitude, follow it." — William James

97. "Any fact facing us is not as important as our attitude toward it, for that determines our success or failure. The way you think about a fact may defeat you before you ever do anything about it. You are overcome by the fact because you think you are." - Norman Vincent Peale

98. "Your living is determined not so much by what life brings to you as by the attitude you bring to life; not so much by what happens to you as by the way your mind looks at what happens." - Kahlil Gibran

99. "Ability is what you're capable of doing. Motivation determines what you do. Attitude determines how well you do it." - Lou Holtz

100. "You cannot control what happens to you, but you can control your attitude toward what happens to you, and in that, you will be mastering change rather than allowing it to master you." - Brian Tracy

101. "Attitude is a little thing that makes a big difference." - Winston Churchill

102. "Your attitude, not your aptitude, will determine your altitude" - Zig Ziglar

103. "The meaning of things lies not in the things themselves, but in our attitude towards them." - Antoine de Saint-Exupery

104. "Our attitude toward life determines life's attitude towards us." - John N. Mitchell

105. "Any fact facing us is not as important as our attitude toward it, for that determines our success or failure" - Norman Vincent Peale

106. "We cannot change our past. We cannot change the fact that people act in a certain way. We cannot change the inevitable. The only thing we can do is play on the one string we have, and that is our attitude." - Charles R. Swindoll

107. "The greatest discovery of any generation is that a human being can alter his life by altering his attitude." - William James

108. "Happiness doesn't depend on any external conditions; it is governed by our mental attitude" - Dale Carnegie

109. "The one thing you can't take away from me is the way I choose to respond to what you do to me. The last of one's freedoms is to choose ones attitude in any given circumstance." - Viktor Frankl

110. "Your living is determined not so much by what life brings to you as by the attitude you bring to life; not so much by what happens to you as by the way your mind looks at what happens." - Kahlil Gibran

111. "Whenever you're in conflict with someone, there is one factor that can make the difference between damaging your relationship and deepening it. That factor is attitude." - William James

112. "There is little difference in people, but that little difference makes a big difference. The little difference is attitude. The big difference is whether it is positive or negative." - W. Clement Stone

113. "Attitudes are nothing more than habits of thoughts, and habits can be acquired. An action repeated becomes an attitude realized." - Paul Myer

114. "Attitude is more important than the past, than education, than money, than circumstances, than what people do or say. It is more important than appearance, giftedness, or skill." - W. C. Fields

115. "Nothing can stop the man with the right mental attitude from achieving his goal; nothing on earth can help the man with the wrong mental attitude." - Thomas Jefferson

116. "I believe the single most significant decision I can make on a day-to-day basis is my choice of attitude. It is more important than my past, my education, my bankroll, my successes or failures, fame or pain, what other people think of me or say about me, my circumstances, or my position. Attitude keeps me going or cripples my progress. It alone fuels my fire or assaults my hope. When my attitudes are right, there is no barrier too high, no valley too deep, no dream too extreme, no challenge too great for me." - Charles R. Swindoll

117. "If you don't like something, change it. If you can't change it, change your attitude."
- Maya Angelou

118. "A positive attitude may not solve every problem but it makes solving any problem a more pleasant experience." - Grant Fairley

119. "It is our attitude at the beginning of a difficult undertaking which, more than anything else, will determine its successful outcome." - William James

120. "For success, attitude is equally as important as ability." - Harry F. Banks

121. "A conviction of self-worth and passion for ideals fuse in a life attitude that is positive, free, noble and spiritually enhancing." - Bill Jay

122. "It is very important to generate a good attitude, a good heart, as much as possible. From this, happiness in both the short term and the long term for both yourself and others will come." - Dalai Lama

123. "Excellence is not a skill. It is an attitude." - Ralph Marston

CHANGE

124. "Action and reaction, ebb and flow, trial and error, change - this is the rhythm of living. Out of our over-confidence, fear; out of our fear, clearer vision, fresh hope. And out of hope, progress."   - Bruce Barton

125. "All changes, even the most longed for, have their melancholy; for what we leave behind us is a part of ourselves; we must die to one life before we can enter another. " - Anatole France

126. "Always remember that the future comes one day at a time. " - Dean Acheson

127. "Any change, even a change for the better, is always accompanied by drawbacks and discomforts. " - Arnold Bennett

128. "He that will not apply new remedies must expect new evils; for time is the greatest innovator. " -   Francis Bacon

129. "He who rejects change is the architect of decay. The only human institution which rejects progress is the cemetery. " - Harold Wilson

130. "If there is anything that we wish to change in the child, we should first examine it and see whether it is not something that could better be changed in ourselves." - Carl Jung

131. "If there is no struggle, there is no progress. " - Frederick Douglass

132. "If we don't change, we don't grow. If we don't grow, we aren't really living. " - Gail Sheehy

133. "If you don't like something, change it. If you can't change it, change your attitude. " - Maya Angelou

134. "It's the most unhappy people who most fear change. " - Mignon McLaughlin

135. "Life belongs to the living, and he who lives must be prepared for changes. " - Johann Wolfgang von Goethe

136. "The world hates change, yet it is the only thing that has brought progress. " - Charles Kettering

137. "They must often change, who would be constant in happiness or wisdom. " - Confucius

138. "Things alter for the worse spontaneously, if they be not altered for the better designedly. "- Francis Bacon

139. "Things do not change; we change. " - Henry David Thoreau

140. "Without change, something sleeps inside us, and seldom awakens. The sleeper must awaken. " - Frank Herbert

141. "If you don't like something change it; if you can't change it, change the way you think about it." - Mary Engelbreit

142. "When we are no longer able to change a situation, we are challenged to change ourselves." - Victor Frankl

143. "Change always comes bearing gifts." - Price Pritchett

144. "The only difference between a rut and a grave is their dimensions." - Ellen Glasgow

145. "Growth is the only evidence of life." - John Henry Newman

146. "Time is a dressmaker specializing in alterations." - Faith Baldwin

147. "The circumstances of the world are so variable that an irrevocable purpose or opinion is almost synonymous with a foolish one." - William H. Seward

148. "The birds are molting. If only man could molt also - his mind once a year its errors, his heart once a year its useless passions." - James Allen

149. "The man who never alters his opinion is like standing water, and breeds reptiles of the mind." - William Blake

150. "What you have become is the price you paid to get what you used to want." - Mignon McLaughlin

151. "Those who expect moments of change to be comfortable and free of conflict have not learned their history." - Joan Wallach Scott

152. "After you've done a thing the same way for two years, look it over carefully.   After five years, look at it with suspicion.   And after ten years, throw it away and start all over."   - Alfred Edward Perlman

153. "Continuity gives us roots; change gives us branches, letting us stretch and grow and reach new heights."   - Pauline R. Kezer

154. "If you would attain to what you are not yet, you must always be displeased by what you are.   For where you are pleased with yourself there you have remained.   Keep adding, keep walking, keep advancing." - Saint Augustine

155. "A good question is never answered.   It is not a bolt to be tightened into place but a seed to be planted and to bear more seed toward the hope of greening the landscape of idea."   - John Ciardi

156. "Every beginning is a consequence - every beginning ends something."   - Paul Valery

157. "God grant me the serenity to accept the people I cannot change, the courage to change the one I can, and the wisdom to know it's me." - unknown

158. "Neither a wise man nor a brave man lies down on the tracks of history to wait for the train of the future to run over him." - Dwight D. Eisenhower

159. "The only man I know who behaves sensibly is my tailor; he takes my measurements anew each time he sees me. The rest go on with their old measurements and expect me to fit them." - George Bernard Shaw

CHOICE

160. "Every human has four endowments-self awareness, conscience, independent will and creative imagination. These give us the ultimate human freedom... The power to choose, to respond, to change." - Stephen R. Covey

161. "By choosing not to allow parts of ourselves to exist, we are forced to expend huge amounts of psychic energy to keep them beneath the surface. " - Debbie Ford

162. "Your life is the sum result of all the choices you make, both consciously and unconsciously. If you can control the process of choosing, you can take control of all aspects of your life. You can find the freedom that comes from being in charge of yourself." - Robert F. Bennett

163. "It's choice--not chance--that determines your destiny." - Jean Nidetch

164. "There is a point at which everything becomes simple and there is no longer any question of choice, because all you have staked will be lost if you look back. Life's point of no return." - Dag Hammarskjold

165. "Be miserable. Or motivate yourself. Whatever has to be done, it's always your choice." - Wayne Dyer

166. "Choose your love, Love your choice." - Thomas S. Monson

167. "Every choice moves us closer to or farther away from something. Where are your choices taking your life? What do your behaviors demonstrate that you are saying yes or no to in life?" - Eric Allenbaugh

168. "There are three constants in life... change, choice and principles." - Stephen R. Covey

169. "Every man builds his world in his own image. He has the power to choose, but no power to escape the necessity of choice." - Ayn Rand

170. "When you have to make a choice and don't make it, that is in itself a choice." - William James

171. "Every choice you make has an end result." - Zig Ziglar

172. "The remarkable thing is, we have a choice everyday regarding the attitude we will embrace for that day." - Charles R. Swindoll

173. "The strongest principle of growth lies in human choice." - George Eliot

174. "Man is unique in that he has plans, purpose and goals which require the need for criteria of choice. The need for ethical value is within man whose future may largely be determined by the choice he make" - George Bernard Shaw

175. "The self is not something ready-made, but something in continuous formation through choice of action." - John Dewey

176. "Destiny is no matter of chance. It is a matter of choice: It is not a thing to be waited for, it is a thing to be achieved." - William Jennings Bryan

177. "We choose what attitudes we have right now. And it's a continuing choice." - John Maxwell

178. "You and I are essentially infinite choice-makers. In every moment of our existence, we are in that field of all possibilities where we have access to an infinity of choices." - Deepak Chopra

179. "The strongest principle of growth lies in the human choice." - George Eliot
180. "It is your own convictions which compels you; that is, choice compels choice." – Epictetus

CONFIDENCE

181. "People who ask confidently get more than those who are hesitant and uncertain. When you've figured out what you want to ask for, do it with certainty, boldness and confidence." - Jack Canfield

182. "The greatest waste in the world is the difference between what we are and what we could become." -Ben Herbster

183. "Your past is not your potential. In any hour you can choose to liberate the future." -Marilyn Ferguson

184. "Questions provide the key to unlocking our unlimited potential." - Anthony Robbins

185. "We all have possibilities we don't know about. We can do things we don't even dream we can do." - Dale Carnegie

186. "Our society nurtures the illusion that all the rewards go to the people who are perfect. But many of us are finding out that trying to be perfect is costly." - Debbie Ford

187. "Everything you need you already have. You are complete right now, you are a whole, total person, not an apprentice person on the way to someplace else. Your completeness must be understood by you and experienced in your thoughts as your own personal reality." - Wayne Dyer

188. "Confidence comes not from always being right but from not fearing to be wrong." - Peter T. Mcintyre

189. "The man of genius inspires us with a boundless confidence in our own powers." - Ralph Waldo Emerson

190. "I was always looking outside myself for strength and confidence but it comes from within. It is there all the time." - Anna Freud

191. "Count your blessings. Once you realize how valuable you are and how much you have going for you, the smiles will return, the sun will break out, the music will play, and you will finally be able to move forward the life that God intended for you with grace, strength, courage, and confidence." - Og Mandino

192. "Don't back down just to keep the peace. Standing up for your beliefs builds self-confidence and self-esteem." - Oprah Winfrey

193. "All you need in this life is ignorance and confidence, and then success is sure." - Mark Twain

194. "When you're a beautiful person on the inside, there is nothing in the world that can change that about you. Jealousy is the result of one's lack of self-confidence, self-worth, and self-acceptance. The Lesson: If you can't accept yourself, then certainly no one else will." - Sasha Azevedo

195. "Confidence is going after Moby Dick in a rowboat and taking the tartar sauce with you." - Zig Ziglar

196. "Experience tells you what to do; confidence allows you to do it." - Stan Smith

197. "To succeed in life, you need two things: ignorance and confidence." - Mark Twain

198. "Who has confidence in himself will gain the confidence of others." - Leib Lazarow

199. "Whatever we expect with confidence becomes our own self-fulfilling prophecy." - Brian Tracy

200. "With realization of one's own potential and self-confidence in one's ability, one can build a better world." - Dalai Lama

201. "Believe in yourself! Have faith in your abilities! Without a humble but reasonable confidence in your own powers you cannot be successful or happy." - Norman Vincent Peale

202. "Life is not easy for any of us. But what of that? We must have perseverance and above all confidence in ourselves. We must believe that we are gifted for something, and that this thing, at whatever cost, must be attained." - Marie Curie

203. "If you have no confidence in self, you are twice defeated in the race of life. With confidence, you have won even before you have started." - Marcus Tullius Cicero

204. "Confidence is contagious; so is lack of confidence" - Vince Lombardi

205. "Guts are a combination of confidence, courage, conviction, strength of character, stick-to-itiveness, pugnaciousness, backbone, and intestinal fortitude. They are mandatory for anyone who wants to get to and stay at the top." - D. A. Benton

206. "One important key to success is self-confidence. An important key to self-confidence is preparation." - Arthur Ashe

207. "Nothing builds self-esteem and self-confidence like accomplishment." - Thomas Carlyle

208. "The history of the world is full of men who rose to leadership, by sheer force of self-confidence, bravery and tenacity." - Mahatma Gandhi

209. "There can be no failure to a man who has not lost his courage, his character, his self-respect, or his self-confidence. He is still a King." - Orison Swett Marden

210. "Confidence is that feeling by which the mind embarks in great and honorable courses with a sure hope and trust in itself." - Marcus Tullius Cicero

211. "Self-confidence is the first requisite to great undertakings." - Samuel Johnson

212. "As is our confidence, so is our capacity." - William Hazlitt

213. "Confidence... thrives on honesty, on honor, on the sacredness of obligations, on faithful protection and on unselfish performance. Without them it cannot live." - Franklin D. Roosevelt

214. "If I have lost confidence in myself, I have the universe against me." - Ralph Waldo Emerson

215. "Health is the greatest possession. Contentment is the greatest treasure. Confidence is the greatest friend. Non-being is the greatest joy." - Lao Tzu

DECISION

216. "It's in your moments of decision that your destiny is shaped." - Anthony Robbins

217. "Everything is something you decide to do, and there is nothing you have to do." - Denis Waitley

218. "The best years of your life are the ones in which you decide your problems are your own. You do not blame them on your mother, the ecology, or the president. You realize that you control your own destiny." - Albert Ellis

219. "The possibilities are numerous once we decide to act and not react." - George Bernard Shaw

220. "Each player must accept the cards life deals him or her: but once they are in hand, he or she alone must decide how to play the cards in order to win the game." - Voltaire

221. "Decide that you want it more than you are afraid of it." - Bill Cosby

222. "Build this day on a foundation of pleasant thoughts. Never fret at any imperfections that you fear may impede your progress. Remind yourself, as often as necessary, that you are a creature of God and have the power to achieve any dream by lifting up your thoughts. You can fly when you decide that you can. Never consider yourself defeated again. Let the vision in your heart be in your life's blueprint. Smile!" - Og Mandino

223. "You are the person who has to decide. Whether you'll do it or toss it aside; You are the person who makes up your mind. Whether you'll lead or will linger behind. Whether you'll try for the goal that's afar. Or just be contented to stay where you are." - Edgar A. Guest

224. "The only person you are destined to become is the person you decide to be." - Ralph Waldo Emerson

225. "Whatever course you decide upon, there is always someone to tell you that you are wrong. There are always difficulties arising which tempt you to believe that your critics are right. To map out a course of action and follow it to an end requires courage." - Ralph Waldo Emerson

226. "Nothing is more difficult, and therefore more precious, than to be able to decide." - Napoleon Bonaparte

227. "The happiest people are those who think the most interesting thoughts. Those who decide to use leisure as a means of mental development, who love good music, good books, good pictures, good company, good conversation, are the happiest people in the world. And they are not only happy in themselves, they are the cause of happiness in others." - William Lyon Phelps

228. "Each of you, for himself, by himself and on his own responsibility, must speak. And it is a solemn and weighty responsibility, and not lightly to be flung aside at the bullying of pulpit, press, government, or the empty catchphrases of politicians. Each must for himself alone decide what is right and what is wrong, and which course is patriotic and which isn't. You cannot shirk this and be a man. To decide against your convictions is to be an unqualified and inexcusable traitor, both to yourself and to your country, let man label you as they may. If you alone of all the nation shall decide one way, and that way be the right way according to your convictions of the right, you have done your duty by yourself and by your country- hold up your head! You have nothing to be ashamed of." - Mark Twain

229. "There are two ways of being happy: We must either diminish our wants or augment our means - either may do - the result is the same and it is for each man to decide for himself and to do that which happens to be easier." - Benjamin Franklin

230. "You can't ask for what you want unless you know what it is. A lot of people don't know what they want or they want much less than they deserve. First you have figure out what you want. Second, you have to decide that you deserve it. Third, you have to believe you can get it. And, fourth, you have to have the guts to ask for it." - Barbara De Angelis

231. "The best day of your life is the one on which you decide your life is your own. No apologies or excuses. No one to lean on, rely on, or blame. The gift is yours - it is an amazing journey - and you alone are responsible for the quality of it. This is the day your life really begins." - Bob Moawad

232. ""There Is A Voice Inside Of You, That Whispers All Day Long, "I Feel That This Is Right For Me, I Know That This Is Wrong." No Teacher, Preacher, Parent, Friend Or Wise Man Can Decide What's Right For You- Just Listen To The Voice That Speaks Inside."" - Shel Silverstein

233. "Our ultimate freedom is the right and power to decide how anybody or anything outside ourselves will affect us." - Stephen R. Covey

234. "Decide what you want, decide what you are willing to exchange for it. Establish your priorities and go to work." - H. L. Hunt

235. "You are always a valuable, worthwhile human being -- not because anybody says so, not because you're successful, not because you make a lot of money -- but because you decide to believe it and for no other reason." - Wayne Dyer

236. "When we least expect it, life sets us a challenge to test our courage and willingness to change; at such a moment, there is no point in pretending that nothing has happened or in saying that we are not ready. The challenge will not wait. Life does not look back. A week is more than enough time for us to decide whether or not to accept our destiny." - Paulo Coelho

237. "Every noble work is bound to face problems and obstacles. It is important to check your goal and motivation thoroughly. One should be very truthful, honest, and reasonable. One's actions should be good for others, and for oneself as well. Once a positive goal is chosen, you should decide to pursue it all the way to the end. Even if it is not realized, at least there will be no regret." - Dalai Lama

238. "Every man must decide whether he will walk in the light of creative altruism or in the darkness of destructive selfishness." - Martin Luther King, Jr.

239. "You have brains in your head. You have feet in your shoes. You can steer yourself in any direction you choose. You're on your own. And you know what you know. You are the guy who'll decide where to go." - Dr. Seuss 240. "Our power is in our ability to decide." - Richard Buckminster Fuller

241. "I've continued to recognize the power individuals have to change virtually anything and everything in their lives in an instant. I've learned that the resources we need to turn our dreams into reality are within us, merely waiting for the day when we decide to wake up and claim our birthright." - Anthony Robbins

242. "It does not take much strength to do things, but it requires great strength to decide on what to do." - Elbert Hubbard

243. "If your head tells you one thing, and your heart tells you another, before you do anything, you should first decide whether you have a better head or a better heart" - Marilyn vos Savant

244. "Keep true, never be ashamed of doing right; decide on what you think is right and stick to it." - T.S. Eliot

245. "If you raise your children to feel that they can accomplish any goal or task they decide upon, you will have succeeded as a parent and you will have given your children the greatest of all blessings." - Brian Tracy

246. "Man is a being with free will; therefore, each man is potentially good or evil, and it's up to him and only him (through his reasoning mind) to decide which he wants to be." - Ayn Rand

247. "The day you decide to do it is your lucky day" - Japanese Proverb

248. "Everything starts with yourself / with you making up your mind about what you're going to do with your life. I tell kids that it's a cruel world, and that the world will bend them either left or right, and it's up to them to decide which way to bend." - Tony Dorsett

249. "Every man gotta right to decide his own destiny." - Bob Marley

250. "The most difficult thing is the decision to act, the rest is merely tenacity. The fears are paper tigers. You can do anything you decide to do. You can act to change and control your life; and the procedure, the process is its own reward." - Amelia Earhart

DESIRE

251. "The only place where your dream becomes impossible is in your own thinking." - Robert H. Schuller

252. "Dream no small dreams for they have no power to move the hearts of men." - Goethe

253. "Your hopes, dreams and aspirations are legitimate. They are trying to take you airborne, above the clouds, above the storms, if you only let them." - William James

254. "The desire of gold is not for gold. It is for the means of freedom and benefit." - Ralph Waldo Emerson

255. "Without a sense of urgency, desire loses its value." - Jim Rohn

256. "Out of need springs desire, and out of desire springs the energy and the will to win." - Denis Waitley

257. "The first principle of success is desire - knowing what you want. Desire is the planting of your seed." - Robert Collier

258. "There is one quality which one must possess to win, and that is definiteness of purpose, the knowledge of what one wants, and a burning desire to possess it." - Napoleon Hill

259. "You can have anything you want - if you want it badly enough. You can be anything you want to be, do anything you set out to accomplish if you hold to that desire with singleness of purpose." - Abraham Lincoln

260. "The starting point of all achievement is desire" - Napoleon Hill

261. "Whatever you vividly imagine, ardently desire, sincerely believe, and enthusiastically act upon must inevitably come to pass." - Paul J. Meyer

262. "Human behavior flows from three main sources: desire, emotion, and knowledge" - Plato

263. "Reduce your plan to writing. The moment you complete this, you will have definitely given concrete form to the intangible desire." - Napoleon Hill

264. "Plant the seed of desire in your mind and it forms a nucleus with power to attract to itself everything needed for its fulfillment." - Robert Collier

265. "Create a definite plan for carrying out your desire and begin at once, whether you ready or not, to put this plan into action." - Napoleon Hill

266. "The key to success is to focus our conscious mind on things we desire not things we fear." - Brian Tracy

267. "The more you seek security, the less of it you have. But the more you seek opportunity, the more likely it is that you will achieve the security that you desire." - Brian Tracy

268. "The desire of gold is not for gold. It is for the means of freedom and benefit." - Ralph Waldo Emerson

269. "Thoughts mixed with definiteness of purpose, persistence, and a burning desire are powerful things." - Napoleon Hill

270. "There is a desire deep within the soul which drives man from the seen to the unseen, to philosophy and to the divine" - Kahlil Gibran

271. "A creative man is motivated by the desire to achieve, not by the desire to beat others" - Ayn Rand

272. "Focus more on your desire than on your doubt, and the dream will take care of itself. You may be surprised at how easily this happens. Your doubts are not as powerful as your desires, unless you make them so." - Marcia Wieder

273. "Boredom: the desire for desires" - Leo Nikolaevich Tolstoy

274. "To desire and strive to be of some service to the world, to aim at doing something which shall really increase the happiness and welfare and virtue of mankind - this is a choice which is possible for all of us; and surely it is a good haven to sail for." - Henry Van Dyke

275. "Imagination is the beginning of creation. You imagine what you desire, you will what you imagine and at last you create what you will." - George Bernard Shaw

276. "Burning desire to be or do something gives us staying power - a reason to get up every morning or to pick ourselves up and start in again after a disappointment" - Marsha Sinetar

277. "When you discover your mission, you will feel its demand. It will fill you with enthusiasm and a burning desire to get to work on it." - W. Clement Stone

278. "One great question underlies our experience, whether we think about it or not: what is the purpose of life? From the moment of birth every human being wants happiness and does not want suffering. Neither social conditioning nor education nor ideology affects this. From the very core of our being, we simply desire contentment. Therefore, it is important to discover what will bring about the greatest degree of happiness" - Dalai Lama

279. "If you greatly desire something, have the guts to stake everything on obtaining it." - Brendan Francis

280. "You will become as small as your controlling desire; as great as your dominant aspiration" - James Allen

281. "Those who desire to give up freedom in order to gain security will not have, nor do they deserve, either one." - Benjamin Franklin

282. "When you love people and have the desire to make a profound, positive impact upon the world, then will you have accomplished the meaning to live." - Sasha Azevedo

283. "The desire is thy prayers; and if thy desire is without ceasing, thy prayer will also be without ceasing. The continuance of your longing is the continuance of your prayer." - Saint Augustine

284. "Everything is perfect in the universe - even your desire to improve it." - Wayne Dyer

285. "It is for us to pray not for tasks equal to our powers, but for powers equal to our tasks, to go forward with a great desire forever beating at the door of our hearts as we travel toward our distant goal." - Helen Keller

286. "Image creates desire. You will what you imagine." - J. G. Gallimore

287. "Happiness can be defined, in part at least, as the fruit of the desire and ability to sacrifice what we want now for what we want eventually" - Stephen R. Covey

288. "The will to win, the desire to succeed, the urge to reach your full potential... these are the keys that will unlock the door to personal excellence." - Confucius

289. "One of the most difficult things everyone has to learn is that for your entire life you must keep fighting and adjusting if you hope to survive. No matter who you are or what your position is you must keep fighting for whatever it is you desire to achieve." - George Allen

DREAMS

290. "Believe in your dreams and they may come true; believe in yourself and they will come true" - Unknown

291. "Consult not your fears but your hopes and your dreams. Think not about your frustrations, but about your unfulfilled potential. Concern yourself not with what you tried and failed in, but with what it is still possible for you to do." - Pope John XXIII

292. "Happy are those who dream dreams and are ready to pay the price to make them come true." - Leon Joseph Cardinal Suenens

293. "We grow by our dreams." - Woodrow T. Wilson

294. "There is hope in dreams, imagination, and in the courage of those who wish to make those dreams a reality." - Jonas Salk

295. "Cherish your visions and your dreams as they are the children of your soul; the blueprints of your ultimate achievements." - Napoleon Hill

296. "Dreams are illustrations... from the book your soul is writing about you." - Marsha Norman

297. "We all have our time machines. Some take us back, they're called memories. Some take us forward, they're called dreams." - Jeremy Irons

298. "Dreams do come true, if we only wish hard enough. You can have anything in life if you will sacrifice everything else for it." - James Matthew Barrie

299. "The only thing that will stop you from fulfilling your dreams is you." - Tom Bradley

300. "Dreams are today's answers to tomorrow's questions." - Edgar Cayce

301. "If one advances confidently in the direction of one's dreams, and endeavors to live the life which one has imagined, one will meet with a success unexpected in common hours." - Henry David Thoreau

302. "Somewhere over the rainbow, skies are blue, and the dreams that you dare to dream really do come true" - Lyman Frank Baum

303. "The victory of success is half won when one gains the habit of setting goals and achieving them. Even the most tedious chore will become endurable as you parade through each day convinced that every task, no matter how menial or boring, brings you closer to fulfilling your dreams." - Og Mandino

304. "Your vision will become clear only when you look into your heart. Who looks outside, dreams. Who looks inside, awakens." - Carl Gustav Jung

305. "Be careful what you water your dreams with. Water them with worry and fear and you will produce weeds that choke the life from your dream. Water them with optimism and solutions and you will cultivate success. Always be on the lookout for ways to turn a problem into an opportunity for success. Always be on the lookout for ways to nurture your dream." - Lao Tzu

306. "You're in the midst of a war: a battle between the limits of a crowd seeking the surrender of your dreams, and the power of your true vision to create and contribute. It is a fight between those who will tell you what you cannot do, and that part of you that knows / and has always known / that we are more than our environment; and that a dream, backed by an unrelenting will to attain it, is truly a reality with an imminent arrival." - Anthony Robbins

307. "Trust in dreams, for in them is hidden the gate to eternity." - Kahlil Gibran

308. "Dreams and dedication are a powerful combination." - William Longgood

309. "I prefer to be a dreamer among the humblest, with visions to be realized, than lord among those without dreams and desires." - Kahlil Gibran

310. "We dance for laughter, we dance for tears, we dance for madness, we dance for fears, we dance for hopes, we dance for screams, we are the dancers, we create the dreams." - unknown

311. "You have to dream before your dreams can come true." - Abdul Kalam

312. "Even the wildest dreams have to start somewhere. Allow yourself the time and space to let your mind wander and your imagination fly." - Oprah Winfrey

313. "The best reason for having dreams is that in dreams no reasons are necessary." - Ashleigh Brilliant

314. "I believe that imagination is stronger than knowledge - myth is more potent than history - dreams are more powerful than facts - hope always triumphs over experience - laughter is the cure for grief - love is stronger than death" - Robert Fulghum

315. "Dreams pass into the reality of action. From the actions stems the dream again; and this interdependence produces the highest form of living." - Anais Nin

316. "A fool dreams of wealth; a wise man, of happiness." - Turkish Proverb

FAITH

317. "If you can conceive it in your mind, then it can be brought to the physical world." - Bob Proctor

318. "Faith is not belief without proof, but trust without reservation." - unknown

319. "Faith... is the art of holding on to things your reason once accepted, despite your changing moods." - C.S. Lewis

320. "When you have come to the edge of all light that you know and are about to drop off into the darkness of the unknown, Faith is knowing One of two things will happen: There will be something solid to stand on or You will be taught to fly" - Patrick Overton

321. "The only thing that stands between a man and what he wants from life is often merely the will to try it and the faith to believe that it is possible." - David Viscott

322. "Everything you are seeking are seeking you in return. Therefore, everything you want is already yours. So, you don't have to get anything. It is simply a matter of becoming more aware of what you already possess." - Bob Proctor

323. "The reason birds can fly and we can't is simply that they have perfect faith, for to have faith is to have wings" - James Matthew Barrie

324. "You block your dream when you allow your fear to grow bigger than your faith." - Mary Manin Morrissey

325. "To one who has faith, no explanation is necessary. To one without faith, no explanation is possible." - St. Thomas Aquinas

326. "Thoughts become things. If you see it in your mind, you will hold it in your hand." - Bob Proctor

327. "Faith consists in believing when it is beyond the power of reason to believe." - Voltaire

328. "Just as the body cannot exist without blood, so the soul needs the matchless and pure strength of faith" - Mahatma Gandhi

329. "The man who cannot believe in himself cannot believe in anything else. The basis of all integrity and character is whatever faith we have in our own integrity." - Roy L. Smith

330. "The only limits in our life are those we impose on ourselves." - Bob Proctor

331. "The smallest seed of faith is better than the largest fruit of happiness." - Henry David Thoreau

332. "Skepticism is the beginning of Faith." - Oscar Wilde

333. "If you can envision it, you can have it!" - Bob Proctor

334. "I do believe that when we face challenges in life that are far beyond our own power, it's an opportunity to build on our faith, inner strength, and courage. I've learned that how we face challenges plays a big role in the outcome of them." - Sasha Azevedo

335. "Each of us has an inner dream that we can unfold if we will just have the courage to admit what it is. And the faith to trust our own admission. The admitting is often very difficult." - Julia Cameron

336. "Faith is to believe what you do not see; the reward of this faith is to see what you believe." - Saint Augustine

337. "Faith is a knowledge within the heart, beyond the reach of proof." - Kahlil Gibran

338. "As your faith is strengthened you will find that there is no longer the need to have a sense of control, that things will flow as they will, and that you will flow with them, to your great delight and benefit." - Emmanuel Teney

339. "Faith is a process of leaping into the abyss not on the basis of any certainty about ~where~ we shall land, but rather on the belief that we ~shall~ land." - Carter Heyward

340. "Faith sees a beautiful blossom in a bulb, a lovely garden in a seed, and a giant oak in an acorn." - William Arthur Ward

341. "Faith is not something to grasp, it is a state to grow into." - Mahatma Gandhi

342. "Painting is a faith, and it imposes the duty to disregard public opinion." - Vincent van Gogh

343. "A faith to live by, a self to live with, and a purpose to live for." - Bob Harrington

344. "Faith is taking the first step even when you don't see the whole staircase." - Martin Luther King, Jr.

345. "Faith is not belief. Belief is passive. Faith is active." - Edith Hamilton

346. "Faith is the daring of the soul to go farther than it can see" - William Newton Clarke

347. "The foundation stones for a balanced success are honesty, character, integrity, faith, love and loyalty." - Zig Ziglar

348. "A faith is a necessity to a man. Woe to him who believes in nothing." - Victor Hugo

349. "There is but one cause of human failure. And that is man's lack of faith in his true Self." - William James

350. "In faith there is enough light for those who want to believe and enough shadows to blind those who don't." - Blaise Pascal

351. "There are nine requisites for contented living: HEALTH enough to make work a pleasure; WEALTH enough to support your needs; STRENGTH enough to battle with difficulties and forsake them; GRACE enough to confess your sins and overcome them; PATIENCE enough to toil until some good is accomplished; CHARITY enough to see some good in your neighbor; LOVE enough to move you to be useful and helpful to others; FAITH enough to make real the things of God; HOPE enough to remove all anxious fears concerning the future." - Johann Wolfgang von Goethe

352. "Faith is the confidence, the assurance, the enforcing truth, the knowing..." - Robert Collier

353. "On a long journey of human life, faith is the best of companions; it is the best refreshment on the journey; and it is the greatest property." - Buddha

354. "Faith makes the discords of the present the harmonies of the future." - Robert Collyer

355. "All of the great achievers of the past have been visionary figures; they were men and women who projected into the future. They thought of what could be, rather than what already was, and then they moved themselves into action, to bring these things into fruition." - Bob Proctor

356. "When you really want something, and you couple that with an understanding of your nature, of your spiritual being, and the laws that govern you, you will keep going, regardless of what's happened. Nothing will stop you." - Bob Proctor

357. "To believe in the things you can see and touch is no belief at all. But to believe in the unseen is both a triumph and a blessing." - Bob Proctor

358. "You have to believe it's possible and believe in yourself. Because after you've decided what you want, you have to believe it's possible, and possible for you, not just for other people. Then you need to seek out models, mentors, and coaches." - Jack Canfield

359. "There's enough for everyone. If you believe it, if you can see it, if you act from it, it will show up for you. That's the truth" - Michael Beckwith

360. "There are laws of the universe and if you practice them they will respond to you" - Michael Beckwith

361. "Believe in yourself! Have faith in your abilities! Without a humble but reasonable confidence in your own powers you cannot be successful or happy." - Norman Vincent Peale

362. "The real source of wealth and capital in this new era is not material things. it is the human mind, the human spirit, the human imagination, and our faith in the future." - Steve Forbes

363. "Every achiever that I have ever met says, 'My life turned around when I began to believe in me.'" - Dr. Robert H. Schuller

364. "The most valuable things in life are not measured in monetary terms. The really important things are not houses and lands, stocks and bonds, automobiles and real estate, but friendships, trust, confidence, empathy, mercy, love and faith." - Bertrand Russell

FEAR

365. "Most fears cannot withstand the test of careful scrutiny and analysis. When we expose our fears to the light of thoughtful examination they usually just evaporate.' - Jack Canfield

366. "He who is not everyday conquering some fear has not learned the secret of life." - Ralph Waldo Emerson

367. "Let fear be a counselor and not a jailer" - Anthony Robbins

368. "Fear less, hope more; Eat less, chew more; Whine less, breathe more; Talk less, say more; Love more, and all good things will be yours" - Swedish Proverb

369. "Ultimately we know deeply that the other side of every fear is freedom." - Marilyn Ferguson

370. "The whole secret of existence is to have no fear. Never fear what will become of you, depend on no one. Only the moment you reject all help are you freed." - Buddha

371. "The wise man in the storm prays to God, not for safety from danger, but deliverance from fear" - Ralph Waldo Emerson

372. "Courage is resistance to fear, mastery of fear - not absence of fear" - Mark Twain

373. "To overcome a fear, here's all you have to do: realize the fear is there, and do the action you fear anyway." - Peter McWilliams

374. "Procrastination is the fear of success. People procrastinate because they are afraid of the success that they know will result if they move ahead now. Because success is heavy, carries a responsibility with it, it is much easier to procrastinate and live on the 'someday I'll' philosophy." - Denis Waitley

375. "You can conquer almost any fear if you will only make up your mind to do so. For remember, fear doesn't exist anywhere except in the mind." - Dale Carnegie

376. "Fear is the main source of superstition, and one of the main sources of cruelty. To conquer fear is the beginning of wisdom." - Bertrand Russell

377. "Do what you fear, and the death of fear is certain" - Anthony Robbins

378. "Do the thing you fear to do and keep on doing it... that is the quickest and surest way ever yet discovered to conquer fear." - Dale Carnegie

379. "Inaction breeds doubt and fear. Action breeds confidence and courage. If you want to conquer fear, do not sit home and think about it. Go out and get busy." - Dale Carnegie

380. "He who is not everyday conquering some fear has not learned the secret of life." - Ralph Waldo Emerson

381. "If you look into your own heart, and you find nothing wrong there, what is there to worry about? What is there to fear?" - Confucius

382. "Fear is something to be moved through, not something to be turned from." - Peter McWilliams

383. "FEAR is an acronym in the English language for "False Evidence Appearing Real"" - Neale Donald Walsch

384. "Fear is a habit; so is self-pity, defeat, anxiety, despair, hopelessness and resignation. You can eliminate all of these negative habits with two simple resolves: I can!! and I will!!" - unknown

385. "You gain strength, courage, and confidence by every experience in which you really stop to look fear in the face... do the thing you think you cannot do." - Eleanor Roosevelt

386. "He who fears to suffer, suffers from fear" - French Proverb

387. "Do what you fear most and you control fear." - Tom Hopkins

388. "Courage leads to heaven; fear to death" - Seneca

389. "There are four ways you can handle fear. You can go over it, under it, or around it. But if you are ever to put fear behind you, you must walk straight through it. Once you put fear behind you, leave it there." - Donna A. Favors

390. "Courage is not the absence of fear, but rather the judgment that something else is more important than fear." - Ambrose Redmoon

391. "Our deepest fear is not that we are inadequate. Our deepest fear is that we are powerful beyond measure. It is our light, not our darkness, that most frightens us. We ask ourselves, who am I to be brilliant, gorgeous, talented, and fabulous? Actually, who are you not to be? You are a child of God. You playing small doesn't serve the world. There's nothing enlightened about shrinking so that other people won't feel insecure around you. We are all meant to shine, as children do. We are born to make manifest the glory of God that is within us. It's not just in some of us, it's in everyone. And as we let our own light shine, we unconsciously give other people permission to do the same. As we are liberated from our own fear, our presence automatically liberates others." - Marianne Williamson

392. "I must not fear. Fear is the mind-killer. Fear is the little-death that brings total obliteration. I will face my fear... And when it is gone past I will turn the inner eye to see its path. Where the fear is gone there will be nothing. Only I will remain." - Frank Herbert

393. "Since fear is mostly about ignorance, the best part is that it's as temporary as you choose." - Christine Comaford

394. "The world we see that seems so insane is the result of a belief system that is not working. To perceive the world differently, we must be willing to change our belief system, let the past slip away, expand our sense of now, and dissolve the fear in our minds." - William James

395. "I have often been afraid, but I wouldn't give in to it. I made myself act as though I was not afraid, and gradually my fear disappeared." - Theodore Roosevelt

396. "Listen to what you know instead of what you fear." - Richard Bach

397. "Worry is a thin stream of fear trickling through the mind. If encouraged, it cuts a channel into which all other thoughts are drained." - Arthur Somers Roche

398. "Fear an ignorant man more than a lion" - Turkish Proverb

399. "They who have conquered doubt and fear have conquered failure" - James Allen

400. "Normal fear protects us; abnormal fear paralyses us. Normal fear motivates us to improve our individual and collective welfare; abnormal fear constantly poisons and distorts our inner lives. Our problem is not to be rid of fear but, rather to harness and master it." - Martin Luther King, Jr.

401. "Indecision is the seedling of fear" -
Napoleon Hill

FOCUS

402. "It's not what's happening to you now or what has happened in your past that determines who you become. Rather, it's your decisions about what to focus on, what things mean to you, and what you're going to do about them that will determine your ultimate destiny." - Anthony Robbins

403. "It is wise to direct your anger towards problems -- not people; to focus your energies on answers -- not excuses." - William Arthur Ward

404. "When you write down your ideas you automatically focus your full attention on them. Few if any of us can write one thought and think another at the same time. Thus a pencil and paper make excellent concentration tools." - Michael Leboeuf

405. "One reason so few of us achieve what we truly want is that we never direct our focus; we never concentrate our power. Most people dabble their way through life, never deciding to master anything in particular." - Anthony Robbins

406. "Goals provide the energy source that powers our lives. One of the best ways we can get the most from the energy we have is to focus it. That is what goals can do for us; concentrate our energy." - Denis Waitley

407. "Don't dwell on what went wrong. Instead, focus on what to do next. Spend your energies on moving forward toward finding the answer." - Denis Waitley

408. "Goals are a means to an end, not the ultimate purpose of our lives. They are simply a tool to concentrate our focus and move us in a direction. The only reason we really pursue goals is to cause ourselves to expand and grow. Achieving goals by themselves will never make us happy in the long term; it's who you become, as you overcome the obstacles necessary to achieve your goals, that can give you the deepest and most long-lasting sense of fulfillment." - Anthony Robbins

409. "The key to success is to focus our conscious mind on things we desire not things we fear." - Brian Tracy

410. "Focus on your potential instead of your limitations" - Alan Loy McGinnis

411. "You can't depend on your judgment when your imagination is out of focus" - Mark Twain

412. "Most people have no idea of the giant capacity we can immediately command when we focus all of our resources on mastering a single area of our lives." - Anthony Robbins

413. "Life is a train of moods like a string of beads; and as we pass through them they prove to be many colored lenses, which paint the world their own hue, and each shows us only what lies in its own focus." - Ralph Waldo Emerson

414. "Focus more on your desire than on your doubt, and the dream will take care of itself. You may be surprised at how easily this happens. Your doubts are not as powerful as your desires, unless you make them so." - Marcia Wieder

415. "I find hope in the darkest of days, and focus in the brightest. I do not judge the universe." - Dalai Lama

416. "All blame is a waste of time. No matter how much fault you find with another, and regardless of how much you blame him, it will not change you. The only thing blame does is to keep the focus off you when you are looking for external reasons to explain your unhappiness or frustration. You may succeed in making another feel guilty about something by blaming him, but you won't succeed in changing whatever it is about you that is making you unhappy." - Wayne Dyer

417. "It is during our darkest moments that we must focus to see the light." - Aristotle Onassis

418. "You can't depend on your eyes when your imagination is out of focus." - Mark Twain

419. "Focus 90% of your time on solutions and only 10% of your time on problems." - Anthony J. D'Angelo

420. "Rather than denying problems, focus inventively, intentionally on what solutions might look or feel like...Our mind is meant to generate ideas that help us escape circumstantial traps / if we trust it to do so. Naturally, not all hunches are useful. But then you only need a single good idea to solve a problem." - Marsha Sinetar

421. "Your future takes precedence over your past. Focus on your future, rather than on the past." - Gary Ryan Blair

422. "If you want to be truly successful invest in yourself to get the knowledge you need to find your unique factor. When you find it and focus on it and persevere your success will blossom." - Sidney Madwed

423. "We can always choose to perceive things differently. You can focus on what's wrong in your life, or you can focus on what's right." - Marianne Williamson

424. "Both abundance and lack exist simultaneously in our lives, as parallel realities. It is always our conscious choice which secret garden we will tend... when we choose not to focus on what is missing from our lives but are grateful for the abundance that's present / love, health, family, friends, work, the joys of nature and personal pursuits that bring us pleasure / the wasteland of illusion falls away and we experience Heaven on earth." - Sarah Ban Breathnach

425. "Focus on the journey, not the destination. Joy is found not in finishing an activity but in doing it." - Greg Anderson

426. "Concentrate all your thoughts upon the work at hand. The sun's rays do not burn until brought to a focus." - Alexander Graham Bell

427. "A mind at peace, a mind centered and not focused on harming others, is stronger than any physical force in the universe." - Wayne Dyer

428. "When I chased after money, I never had enough. When I got my life on purpose and focused on giving of myself and everything that arrived into my life, then I was prosperous." - Wayne Dyer

429. "When every physical and mental resources is focused, one's power to solve a problem multiplies tremendously." - Norman Vincent Peale

430. "Productivity is never an accident. It is always the result of a commitment to excellence, intelligent planning, and focused effort." - Paul J. Meyer

431. "You must remain focused on your journey to greatness." - Les Brown

432. "Only when your consciousness is totally focused on the moment you are in can you receive whatever gift, lesson, or delight that moment has to offer." - Barbara De Angelis

FORGIVENESS

433. "Resentment is like taking poison and waiting for the other person to die." - Malachy McCourt

434. "Forgiveness is not always easy. At times, it feels more painful than the wound we suffered, to forgive the one that inflicted it. And yet, there is no peace without forgiveness." - Marianne Williamson

435. "The past is over and done and cannot be changed. This is the only moment we can experience." - Louise Hay

436. "Whatever we refuse to recognize about ourselves has a way of rearing its head and making itself known when we least expect it." - Debbie Ford

437. "To understand everything is to forgive everything" - Buddha

438. "I really don't think life is about the I-could-have-beens. Life is only about the I-tried-to-do. I don't mind the failure but I can't imagine that I'd forgive myself if I didn't try." - Nikki Giovanni

439. "To love means loving the unlovable. To forgive means pardoning the unpardonable. Faith means believing the unbelievable. Hope means hoping when everything seems hopeless." - G. K. Chesterton

440. "Love yourself—accept yourself—forgive yourself—and be good to yourself, because without you the rest of us are without a source of many wonderful things." - Leo F. Buscaglia

441. "Flatter me, and I may not believe you. Criticize me, and I may not like you. Ignore me, and I may not forgive you. Encourage me, and I will not forget you. Love me and I may be forced to love you." - William Arthur Ward

442. "To forgive is to set a prisoner free and discover that the prisoner was you." - Lewis B. Smedes

443. "Before you speak, listen. Before you write, think. Before you spend, earn. Before you invest, investigate. Before you criticize, wait. Before you pray, forgive. Before you quit, try. Before you retire, save. Before you die, give." - William Arthur Ward

444. "Do more than belong: participate. Do more than care: help. Do more than believe: practice. Do more than be fair: be kind. Do more than forgive: forget. Do more than dream: work." - William Arthur Ward

445. "The weak can never forgive. Forgiveness is the attribute of the strong." - Mahatma Gandhi

446. "When a deep injury is done us, we never recover until we forgive" - Alan Paton

447. "Forgive yourself for your faults and your mistakes and move on." - Les Brown

448. "Let us forgive each other - only then will we live in peace" - Leo Nikolaevich Tolstoy

449. "Forgiveness does not change the past, but it does enlarge the future." - Paul Boese

450. "Sincere forgiveness isn't colored with expectations that the other person apologizes or change. Don't worry whether or not they finally understand you. Love them and release them. Life feeds back truth to people in its own way and time." - Sara Paddison

451. "Without forgiveness life is governed by an endless cycle of resentment and retaliation" - Roberto Assagioli

452. "True forgiveness is not an action after the fact, it is an attitude with which you enter each moment." - David Ridge

453. "Friendship flourishes at the fountain of forgiveness." - William Arthur Ward

454. "Forgiveness is the key that unlocks the door of resentment and the handcuffs of hate. It is a power that breaks the chains of bitterness and the shackles of selfishness."
- William Arthur Ward

455. "The best thing to give to your enemy is forgiveness; to an opponent, tolerance; to a friend, your heart; to your child, a good example; to a father, deference; to your mother, conduct that will make her proud of you; to yourself, respect; to all men, charity."
- Benjamin Franklin

456. "We achieve inner health only through forgiveness - the forgiveness not only of others but also of ourselves" - Joshua Loth Liebman

457. "Inner peace can be reached only when we practice forgiveness. Forgiveness is letting go of the past, and is therefore the means for correcting our misperceptions." - Gerald Jampolsky

458. "Forgiveness is the economy of the heart... forgiveness saves the expense of anger, the cost of hatred, the waste of spirits."
- Hannah Moore

459. "Forgiveness is the giving, and so the receiving, of life." - George MacDonald

FREINDSHIP

460. "A friend is one of the nicest things you can have, and one of the best things you can be." - Douglas Pagels

461. "Friendship isn't a big thing - it's a million little things." - unknown

462. "A single rose can be my garden... a single friend, my world." - Leo Buscaglia

463. "Only your real friends will tell you when your face is dirty." - Sicilian Proverb

464. "The antidote for fifty enemies is one friend." - Aristotle

465. "In everyone's life, at some time, our inner fire goes out. It is then burst into flame by an encounter with another human being. We should all be thankful for those people who rekindle the inner spirit." - Albert Schweitzer

466. "A loyal friend laughs at your jokes when they're not so good, and sympathizes with your problems when they're not so bad." - Arnold H. Glasgow

467. "The friend is the man who knows all about you, and still likes you." - Elbert Hubbard

468. "If a friend is in trouble, don't annoy him by asking if there is anything you can do. Think up something appropriate and do it." - Edgar Watson Howe

469. "The most I can do for my friend is simply be his friend." - Henry David Thoreau

470. "A true friend never gets in your way unless you happen to be going down." - Arnold Glasow

471. "But if the while I think on thee, dear friend, all losses are restored and sorrows end." - William Shakespeare

472. "The most beautiful discovery true friends make is that they can grow separately without growing apart." - Elisabeth Foley

473. "A friend knows the song in my heart and sings it to me when my memory fails." - Donna Roberts

474. "You can always tell a real friend: when you've made a fool of yourself he doesn't feel you've done a permanent job." - Laurence J. Peter

475. "Friends are those rare people who ask how you are and then wait for the answer." - unknown

476. "A friend is the one who comes in when the whole world has gone out." - Grace Pulpit

477. "Constant use will not wear ragged the fabric of friendship." - Dorothy Parker

478. "The best kind of friend is the one you could sit on a porch with, never saying a word, and walk away feeling like that was the best conversation you've had." - unknown

479. "The language of friendship is not words but meanings." - Henry David Thoreau

480. "A true friend is one who thinks you are a good egg even if you are half-cracked." - unknown

481. "If instead of a gem, or even a flower, we should cast the gift of a loving thought into the heart of a friend, that would be giving as the angels give." - George MacDonald

482. "It takes a long time to grow an old friend." - John Leonard

483. "He who has a thousand friends has not a friend to spare, and he who has one enemy will meet him everywhere." - Ralph Waldo Emerson

484. "We are keenly aware of the faults of our friends, but if they like us enough it doesn't matter." - Mignon McLaughlin

485. "A true friend embosoms freely, advises justly, assists readily, adventures boldly, takes all patiently, defends courageously, and continues a friend unchangeably." - William Penn

486. "A good friend is a connection to life - a tie to the past, a road to the future, the key to sanity in a totally insane world." - Lois Wyse

487. "If you're alone, I'll be your shadow.   If you want to cry, I'll be your shoulder.   If you want a hug, I'll be your pillow. If you need to be happy, I'll be your smile. But anytime you need a friend, I'll just be me." - unknown

488. "A man's growth is seen in the successive choirs of his friends." - Ralph Waldo Emerson

GOALS

489. "Set a goal to achieve something that is so big, so exhilarating that it excites you and scares you at the same time. It must be a goal that is so appealing, so much in line with your spiritual core, that you can't get it out of your mind. If you do not get chills when you set a goal, you're not setting big enough goals." - Bob Proctor

490. "Not in his goals but in his transitions is man great" - Ralph Waldo Emerson

491. "Discipline is the bridge between goals and accomplishment." - Jim Rohn

492. "If you know what to do to reach your goal, it's not a big enough goal." - Bob Proctor

493. "Setting goals is the first step in turning the invisible into the visible." - Anthony Robbins

494. "The victory of success is half won when one gains the habit of setting goals and achieving them. Even the most tedious chore will become endurable as you parade through each day convinced that every task, no matter how menial or boring, brings you closer to fulfilling your dreams." - Og Mandino

495. "People are not lazy. They simply have impotent goals / that is, goals that do not inspire them." - Anthony Robbins

496. "We come this way but once. We can either tiptoe through life and hope we get to death without being badly bruised or we can live a full, complete life achieving our goals and realizing our wildest dreams." - Bob Proctor

497. "Without goals, and plans to reach them, you are like a ship that has set sail with no destination." - Fitzhugh Dodson

498. "Goals are dreams with deadlines." - Diana Scharf Hunt

499. "Your purpose explains what you are doing with your life. Your vision explains how you are living your purpose. Your goals enable you to realize your vision." - Bob Proctor

500. "When it is obvious that the goals cannot be reached, don't adjust the goals, adjust the action steps." - Confucius

501. "Learn from the past, set vivid, detailed goals for the future, and live in the only moment of time over which you have any control: now." - Denis Waitley

502. "In the absence of clearly-defined goals, we become strangely loyal to performing daily trivia until ultimately we become enslaved by it." - Robert Heinlein

503. "The reason most people never reach their goals is that they don't define them, learn about them, or even seriously consider them as believable or achievable. Winners can tell you where they are going, what they plan to do along the way, and who will be sharing the adventure with them." - Denis Waitley

504. "All who have accomplished great things have had a great aim; have fixed their gaze on a goal which was high, one which sometimes seemed impossible." - Orison Swett Marden

505. "Learn to become still. And to take your attention away from what you don't want, and all the emotional charge around it, and place your attention on what you wish to experience" - Michael Beckwith

506. "When you are clear, what you want will show up in your life, and only to the extent you are clear." - Janet Attwood

507. "The reason most people never reach their goals is that they don't define them, learn about them, or even seriously consider them as believable or achievable. Winners can tell you where they are going, what they plan to do along the way, and who will" - Denis Waitley

508. "To have Goals is to have a future, because without goals we will strive for nothing." - Andrew Ridings

509. "Goals provide the energy source that powers our lives. One of the best ways we can get the most from the energy we have is to focus it. That is what goals can do for us; concentrate our energy." - Denis Waitley

510. "Goals are a means to an end, not the ultimate purpose of our lives. They are simply a tool to concentrate our focus and move us in a direction. The only reason we really pursue goals is to cause ourselves to expand and grow. Achieving goals by themselves will never make us happy in the long term; it's who you become, as you overcome the obstacles necessary to achieve your goals, that can give you the deepest and most long-lasting sense of fulfillment." - Anthony Robbins

511. "Man is a goal seeking animal. His life only has meaning if he is reaching out and striving for his goals." - Aristotle

512. "Goals allow you to control the direction of change in your favor." - Brian Tracy

513. "Our goals can only be reached through a vehicle of a plan, in which we must fervently believe, and upon which we must vigorously act. There is no other route to success." - Stephen A. Brennan

514. "The most important thing you can do to achieve your goals is to make sure that as soon as you set them, you immediately begin to create momentum. The most important rules that I ever adopted to help me in achieving my goals were those I learned from a very successful man who taught me to first write down the goal, and then to never leave the site of setting a goal without firs taking some form of positive action toward its attainment." - Anthony Robbins

515. "People with goals succeed because they know where they're going." - Earl Nightingale

516. "Whenever you make a mistake or get knocked down by life, don't look back at it too long. Mistakes are life's way of teaching you. Your capacity for occasional blunders is inseparable from your capacity to reach your goals. No one wins them all, and your failures, when they happen, are just part of your growth. Shake off your blunders. How will you know your limits without an occasional failure? Never quit. Your turn will come." - Og Mandino

517. "You must take action now that will move you towards your goals. Develop a sense of urgency in your life." - H. Jackson Brown, Jr.

518. "Anything inside that immobilizes me, gets in my way, keeps me from my goals, is all mine." - Wayne Dyer

519. "Every single life only becomes great when the individual sets upon a goal or goals which they really believe in, which they can really commit themselves to, which they can put their whole heart and soul into." - Brian Tracy

520. "What you get by achieving your goals is to as important as what you become by achieving your goals." - Zig Ziglar

521. "If I feel depressed I will sing. If I feel sad I will laugh. If I feel ill I will double my labor. If I feel fear I will plunge ahead. If I feel inferior I will wear new garments. If I feel uncertain I will raise my voice. If I feel poverty I will think of wealth to come. If I feel incompetent I will think of past success. If I feel insignificant I will remember my goals. Today I will be the master of my emotions." - Og Mandino

522. "When your goals seem too difficult to reach.... move the posts closer" - Phil Long

523. "Your goals are the road maps that guide you and show you what is possible for your life." - Les Brown

524. "Goals are not only absolutely necessary to motivate us. They are essential to really keep us alive." - Robert H. Schuller

525. "The most important thing about having goals is having one." - Abert F. Geoffrey

526. "You must see your goals clearly and specifically before you can set out for them. Hold them in your mind until they become second nature." - Les Brown

527. "Don't be a time manager, be a priority manager. Cut your major goals into bite-sized pieces. Each small priority or requirement on the way to ultimate goal become a mini goal in itself." - Denis Waitley

528. "You control your future, your destiny. What you think about comes about. By recording your dreams and goals on paper, you set in motion the process of becoming the person you most want to be. Put your future in good hands - your own." - Mark Victor Hansen

529. "If you're bored with life - you don't get up every morning with a burning desire to do things - you don't have enough goals." - Lou Holtz

530. "We are built to conquer environment, solve problems, achieve goals, and we find no real satisfaction or happiness in life without obstacles to conquer and goals to achieve." - Maxwell Maltz

531. "A person should set his goals as early as he can and devote all his energy and talent to getting there. With enough effort, he may achieve it. Or he may find something that is even more rewarding. But in the end, no matter what the outcome, he will know he has been alive." - Walt Disney

GRATITUDE

532. "Let's start with what we can be thankful for, and get our mind into that vibration, and then watch the good that starts to come, because one thought leads to another thought." - by Bob Proctor

533. "Gratitude is an attitude that hooks us up to our source of supply. And the more grateful you are, the closer you become to your maker, to the architect of the universe, to the spiritual core of your being. It's a phenomenal lesson." - Bob Proctor

534. "Let us be grateful to people who make us happy, they are the charming gardeners who make our souls blossom." - Marcel Proust

535. "Let us be grateful to people who make us happy, they are the charming gardeners who make our souls blossom." - Marcel Proust

536. "The enlightened give thanks for what most people take for granted ...... As you begin to be grateful for what most people take for granted, that vibration of gratitude makes you more receptive to good in your life" - Michael Beckwith

537. "Gratitude makes sense of our past, brings peace for today, and creates a vision for tomorrow." - unknown

538. "Gratitude   unlocks the fullness of life. It turns what we have into enough, and more. It turns denial into acceptance, chaos to order, confusion to clarity. It can turn a meal into a feast, a house into a home, a stranger into a friend. Gratitude makes sense of our past, brings peace for today, and creates a vision for tomorrow." - Melody Beattie

539. "At times our own light goes out and is rekindled by a spark from another person. Each of us has cause to think with deep gratitude of those who have lighted the flame within us." - Albert Schweitzer

540. "When you are grateful, fear disappears and abundance appears." - Anthony Robbins

541. "When it comes to life the critical thing is whether you take things for granted or take them with gratitude." - G. K. Chesterton

542. "Feeling gratitude and not expressing it is like wrapping a present and not giving it." - William Arthur Ward

543. "I would maintain that thanks are the highest form of thought, and that gratitude is happiness doubled by wonder." - G. K. Chesterton

544. "As we express our gratitude, we must never forget that the highest appreciation is not to utter words, but to live by them." - John Fitzgerald Kennedy

545. "Develop an attitude of gratitude, and give thanks for everything that happens to you, knowing that every step forward is a step toward achieving something bigger and better than your current situation." - Brian Tracy

546. "Gratitude is when memory is stored in the heart and not in the mind." - Lionel Hampton

547. "No one who achieves success does so without acknowledging the help of others. The wise and confident acknowledge this help with gratitude." - Alfred North Whitehead

548. "I have learned that some of the nicest people you'll ever meet are those who have suffered a traumatic event or loss. I admire them for their strength, but most especially for their life gratitude - a gift often taken for granted by the average person in society." - Sasha Azevedo

549. "Good men and bad men differ radically. Bad men never appreciate kindness shown them, but wise men appreciate and are grateful. Wise men try to express their appreciation and gratitude by some return of kindness, not only to their benefactor, but to everyone else" - Buddha

550. "Gratitude bestows reverence, allowing us to encounter everyday epiphanies, those transcendent moments of awe that change forever how we experience life and the world." - John Milton

551. "Gratitude is a duty which ought to be paid, but which none have a right to expect" - Jean-Jacques Rousseau

552. "God gave you a gift of 86,400 seconds today. Have you used one to say "thank you?"" - William Arthur Ward

553. "If the only prayer you said in your whole life was, "thank you," that would suffice" - Meister Eckhart

554. "The only people with whom you should try to get even are those who have helped you." - John E. Southard

555. "As each day comes to us refreshed and anew, so does my gratitude renew itself daily. The breaking of the sun over the horizon is my grateful heart dawning upon a blessed world." - Terri Guillemets

556. "For each new morning with its light, For rest and shelter of the night, For health and food, for love and friends, For everything Thy goodness sends." - Ralph Waldo Emerson

557. "The unthankful heart... discovers no mercies; but let the thankful heart sweep through the day and, as the magnet finds the iron, so it will find, in every hour, some heavenly blessings!" - Henry Ward Beecher

558. "He is a wise man who does not grieve for the things which he has not, but rejoices for those which he has." - Epictetus

559. "Not what we say about our blessings, but how we use them, is the true measure of our thanksgiving." - W.T. Purkiser

560. "Gratitude is a quality similar to electricity: it must be produced and discharged and used up in order to exist at all." - William Faulkner

561. "If you want to turn your life around, try thankfulness.   It will change your life mightily." - Gerald Good

562. "The hardest arithmetic to master is that which enables us to count our blessings." - Eric Hoffer

HAPPINESS

563. "The happiness of a man in this life does not consist in the absence but in the mastery of his passions." - Alfred Lord Tennyson

564. "A man is not rightly conditioned until he is a happy, healthy, and prosperous being; and happiness, health, and prosperity are the result of a harmonious adjustment of the inner with the outer of the man with his surroundings." - James Allen

565. "Finally, what I really want is to be happy in this moment, where the magic and miracles happen. Stay in the moment and all gifts are added as you breathe and take inspired action." - Joe Vitale

566. "If you want to be happy, set a goal that commands your thoughts, liberates your energy and inspires your hopes." - Andrew Carnegie

567. "If you want to be happy, be." - Leo Tolstoy

568. "Most people would rather be certain they're miserable, than risk being happy." - Robert Anthony

569. "The best way to cheer yourself up is to try to cheer somebody else up." - Mark Twain

570. "Nobody really cares if you're miserable, so you might as well be happy." - Cynthia Nelms

571. "Those who can laugh without cause have either found the true meaning of happiness or have gone stark raving mad." - Norm Papernick

572. "Man is fond of counting his troubles, but he does not count his joys.   If he counted them up as he ought to, he would see that every lot has enough happiness provided for it." - Fyodor Dostoevsky

573. "What a wonderful life I've had!   I only wish I'd realized it sooner." - Colette

574. "The foolish man seeks happiness in the distance; the wise grows it under his feet." - James Openheim

575. "People take different roads seeking fulfillment and happiness.   Just because they're not on your road doesn't mean they've gotten lost." - H. Jackson Browne

576. "Often people attempt to live their lives backwards; they try to have more things, or more money, in order to do more of what they want, so they will be happier.   The way it actually works is the reverse. You must first be who you really are, then do what you need to do, in order to have what you want." - Margaret Young

577. "Happiness is like a butterfly which, when pursued, is always beyond our grasp, but, if you will sit down quietly, may alight upon you." - Nathaniel Hawthorne

578. "It's never too late to have a happy childhood." - Berke Breathed

579. "Happiness?   That's nothing more than health and a poor memory." - Albert Schweitzer

580. "If you want others to be happy, practice compassion. If you want to be happy, practice compassion." - Dalai Lama

581. "Happiness held is the seed; happiness shared is the flower." - unknown

582. "He is rich or poor according to what he is, not according to what he has." - Henry Ward Beecher

583. "If you search the world for happiness, you may find it in the end, for the world is round and will lead you back to your door." - Robert Brault

584. "Cheerfulness is what greases the axles of the world.   Don't go through life creaking." - H.W. Byles

585. "For every minute you are angry you lose sixty seconds of happiness." - Ralph Waldo Emerson

586. "It is not easy to find happiness in ourselves, and it is not possible to find it elsewhere." - Agnes Repplier

587. "Happiness equals reality minus expectations" - Tom Magliozzi

588. "The greatest happiness of life is the conviction that we are loved -- loved for ourselves, or rather, loved in spite of ourselves." - Victor Hugo

589. "There is only one way to happiness and that is to cease worrying about things which are beyond the power of our will." - Epictetus

590. "This very moment is a seed from which the flowers of tomorrow's happiness grow." - Margaret Lindsey

591. "Get happiness out of your work or you may never know what happiness is." - Elbert Hubbard

592. "It is not in doing what you like, but in liking what you do that is the secret of happiness" - James Matthew Barrie

593. "Happiness comes of the capacity to feel deeply, to enjoy simply, to think freely, to risk life, to be needed." - Storm Jameson

594. "Happiness is not something readymade. It comes from your own actions." - Dalai Lama

595. "Happiness is when what you think, what you say, and what you do are in harmony." - Mohandas Gandhi

596. "Success in its highest and noblest form calls for peace of mind and enjoyment and happiness which come only to the man who has found the work that he likes best." - Napoleon Hill

597. "Happiness is not a goal; it is a by-product." - Eleanor Roosevelt

598. "True happiness... is not attained through self-gratification, but through fidelity to a worthy purpose." - Helen Keller

599. "Are you bored with life? Then throw yourself into some work you believe in with all your heart, live for it, die for it, and you will find happiness that you had thought could never be yours." - Dale Carnegie

600. "Happiness makes up in height for what it lacks in length." - Robert Frost

601. "Happiness is not something you postpone for the future; it is something you design for the present." - Jim Rohn

602. "But what is happiness except the simple harmony between a man and the life he leads?" - Albert Camus

603. "There is no value in life except what you choose to place upon it and no happiness in any place except what you bring to it yourself." - Henry David Thoreau

604. "The happiness of your life depends upon the quality of your thoughts: therefore, guard accordingly, and take care that you entertain no notions unsuitable to virtue and reasonable nature." - Marcus Aurelius

605. "Happiness is a continuation of happenings which are not resisted." - Deepak Chopra

606. "The person born with a talent they are meant to use will find their greatest happiness in using it." - Johann Wolfgang von Goethe

607. "There is a difference between happiness and wisdom: he that thinks himself the happiest man is really so; but he that thinks himself the wisest is generally the greatest fool." - Francis Bacon

608. "The happiness of a man in this life does not consist in the absence but in the mastery of his passions." - Alfred Lord Tennyson

609. "Happiness cannot be traveled to, owned, earned, worn or consumed. Happiness is the spiritual experience of living every minute with love, grace, and gratitude." - Denis Waitley

610. "A man is not rightly conditioned until he is a happy, healthy, and prosperous being; and happiness, health, and prosperity are the result of a harmonious adjustment of the inner with the outer of the man with his surroundings." - James Allen

HOPE

611. "Hope is the companion of power, and mother of success; for who so hopes strongly has within him the gift of miracles." - Samuel Smiles

612. "Hope works in these ways: it looks for the good in people instead of harping on the worst; it discovers what can be done instead of grumbling about what cannot; it regards problems, large or small, as opportunities; it pushes ahead when it would be easy to quit; it "lights the candle" instead of "cursing the darkness."" - Anonymous

613. "What seems to us as bitter trials are often blessings in disguise" - Oscar Wilde

614. "Learn from yesterday, live for today, hope for tomorrow." - Albert Einstein

615. "In all things it is better to hope than to despair" - Johann Wolfgang von Goethe

616. "Hope never abandons you; you abandon it" - George Weinberg

617. "Hope is faith holding out its hand in the dark." - George Iles

618. "What oxygen is to the lungs, such is hope to the meaning of life" - Emil Brunner

619. "Hope is the thing with feathers, that perches in the soul, and sings the tune without words, and never stops at all." - Emily Dickinson

620. "Most of the important things in the world have been accomplished by people who have kept on trying when there seemed to be no hope at all." - Dale Carnegie

621. "What would life be if we had no courage to attempt anything?" - Vincent van Gogh

622. "Hope arouses, as nothing else can arouse, a passion for the possible." - William Sloan Coffin

623. "The very least you can do in your life is to figure out what you hope for. And the most you can do is live inside that hope." - Barbara Kingsolver

624. "Once you choose hope, anything's possible." - Christopher Reeve

625. "When the world says, "Give up," Hope whispers, "Try it one more time."" - unknown

626. "The road that is built in hope is more pleasant to the traveler than the road built in despair, even though they both lead to the same destination." - Marian Zimmer Bradley

627. "Hope is the word which God has written on the brow of every man." - Victor Hugo

IMAGINATION

628. "Only as high as I reach can I grow, only as far as I seek can I go, only as deep as I look can I see, only as much as I dream can I be." - Karen Ravn

629. "Every problem has in it the seeds of its own solution. If you don't have any problems, you don't get any seeds." - Norman Vincent Peale

630. "Empty pockets never held anyone back. Only empty heads and empty hearts can do that." - Norman Vincent Peale

631. "We are not human beings on a spiritual journey. We are spiritual beings on a human journey." — Dr. Stephen Covey

632. "Our aspirations are our possibilities." -Robert Browning

633. "Who are we? We are children of God. Our potential is unlimited. Our inheritance is sacred. May we always honor that heritage — in every thought and deed." -Russell M. Nelson

634. "The potential of the average person is like a huge ocean unsailed, a new continent unexplored, a world of possibilities waiting to be released and channeled toward some great good." -Brian Tracy

635. "Humanity has only scratched the surface of its real potential." - Peace Pilgrim

636. "The most common commodity in this country is unrealized potential." - Calvin Coolidge

637. "It is a denial of the divinity within us to deny our potential and possibilities." -James E. Faust

638. "No matter what the level of your ability, you have more potential than you can ever develop in a lifetime." -James T Mccay

639. "The only limits to the possibilities in your life tomorrow are the buts you use today." -Les Brown

640. "You are your own scriptwriter and the play is never finished, no matter what your age or position in life." — Denis Waitley

641. "Living consciously involves being genuine; it involves listening and responding to others honestly and openly; it involves being in the moment." — Sidney Poitier

642. "Life is a great big canvas, and you should throw all the paint on it you can." — Danny Kaye

643. "Imagination is everything. It is the preview of life's coming attractions." - Albert Einstein

644. "If you have zest and enthusiasm you attract zest and enthusiasm. Life does give back in kind." - Norman Vincent Peale

645. "The true sign of intelligence is not knowledge but imagination." - Albert Einstein

646. "Imagination is more important than knowledge. For knowledge is limited to all we now know and understand, while imagination embraces the entire world, and all there ever will be to know and understand." - Albert Einstein

647. "Logic will get you from A to B. Imagination will take you everywhere." - Albert Einstein

648. "Reason can answer questions, but imagination has to ask them." - Dr. Ralph Gerard

649. "Things are pretty, graceful, rich, elegant, handsome, but until they speak to the imagination, not yet beautiful" - Ralph Waldo Emerson

650. "Nothing limits achievement like small thinking; nothing expands possibilities like unleashed imagination." - William Arthur Ward

651. "This world is but a canvas to our imaginations." - Henry David Thoreau

652. "The world of reality has its limits; the world of imagination is boundless." - Jean-Jacques Rousseau

653. "Even the wildest dreams have to start somewhere. Allow yourself the time and space to let your mind wander and your imagination fly." - Oprah Winfrey

654. "The level of our success is limited only by our imagination and no act of kindness, however small, is ever wasted" - Aesop

655. "There is a space between man's imagination and man's attainment that may only be traversed by his longing" - Kahlil Gibran

656. "I believe in the imagination. What I cannot see is infinitely more important than what I can see." - Duane Michals

657. "A rock pile ceases to be a rock pile the moment a single man contemplates it, bearing within him the image of a cathedral." - Antoine de Saint-Exupéry

658. "I saw the angel in the marble and carved until I set him free." - Michelangelo

659. "I like nonsense, it wakes up the brain cells. Fantasy is a necessary ingredient in iving, it's a way of looking at life through the wrong end of a telescope. Which is what I do, and that enables you to laugh at life's realities." - Theodore Geisel

660. "Nothing encourages creativity like the chance to fall flat on one's face." - James D. Finley

661. "My alphabet starts with this letter called yuzz. It's the letter I use to spell yuzz-a-ma-tuzz. You'll be sort of surprised what there is to be found once you go beyond 'Z' and start poking around!" - Dr. Seuss

662. "Think left and think right and think low and think high.   Oh, the thinks you can think up if only you try!" - Dr. Seuss

663. "A fool-proof method for sculpting an elephant: first, get a huge block of marble; then you chip away everything that doesn't look like an elephant." - unknown

664. "The Possible's slow fuse is lit by the Imagination." - Emily Dickinson

665. "I paint objects as I think them, not as I see them." - Pablo Picasso

666. "There are no rules of architecture for a castle in the clouds." - G.K. Chesterton

667. "They who dream by day are cognizant of many things which escape those who dream only by night." - Edgar Allan Poe

668. "Sometimes I've believed as many as six impossible things before breakfast." - Lewis Carroll

669. "Things are only impossible until they're not." - Jean-Luc Picard, Star Trek: The Next Generation

670. "When I have a terrible need of - shall I say the word - religion. Then I go out and paint the stars." - Vincent Van Gogh

671. "In the realist you have the sorry sight of the five senses deprived of their imagination." - Robert Brault

672. "When you are describing, A shape, or sound, or tint; Don't state the matter plainly, But put it in a hint; And learn to look at all things, With a sort of mental squint." - Lewis Carroll

673. "Trust that little voice in your head that says "Wouldn't it be interesting if..."   And then do it." - Duane Michals

674. "It's not what you look at that matters, it's what you see." - Henry David Thoreau

675. "Live out of your imagination, not your history." - Stephen Covey

PASSION

676. "If you're passionate about what it is you do, then you're going to be looking for everything you can to get better at it." - Jack Canfield

677. "The work of art must seize upon you, wrap you up in itself and carry you away. It is the means by which the artist conveys his passion. It is the current which he puts forth, which sweeps you along in his passion" - Pierre-Auguste Renoir

678. "There is no greatness without a passion to be great, whether it's the aspiration of an athlete or an artist, a scientist, a parent or a business person." - Anthony Robbins

679. "A passion for life is one of the most attractive qualities in a human being. If you want a teammate or a life mate who loves to be around you, all you need to do is love to be around." - Denis Waitley

680. "You have to find something that you love enough to be able to take risks, jump over the hurdles and break through the brick walls that are always going to be placed in front of you. If you don't have that kind of feeling for what it is you're doing, you'll stop at the first giant hurdle." — George Lucas

681. "Your profession is not what brings home your paycheck. Your profession is what you were put on earth to do with such passion and such intensity that it becomes spiritual in calling." — Vincent Van Gogh

682. "They may forget what you said, but they will never forget how you made them feel." - Carl W. Buechner

683. "Nothing great in the world has ever been accomplished without passion." - Hebbel

684. "A great leader's courage to fulfill his vision comes from passion, not position." - John Maxwell

685. "Most people are other people. Their thoughts are someone else's opinions, their lives a mimicry, their passions a quotation." - Oscar Wilde

686. "Those who danced were thought to be quite insane by those who could not hear the music." - Angela Monet

687. "The way you get meaning into your life is to devote yourself to loving others, devote yourself to your community around you, and devote yourself to creating something that gives you purpose and meaning." - Mitch Albom

688. "The more intensely we feel about an idea or a goal, the more assuredly the idea, buried deep in our subconscious, will direct us along the path to its fulfillment." - Earl Nightingale

689. "Passion, it lies in all of us, sleeping... waiting... and though unwanted... unbidden... it will stir... open its jaws and howl. It speaks to us... guides us... passion rules us all, and we obey. What other choice do we have? Passion is the source of our finest moments. The joy of love... the clarity of hatred... and the ecstasy of grief. It hurts sometimes more than we can bear. If we could live without passion maybe we'd know some kind of peace... but we would be hollow... Empty rooms shuttered and dank. Without passion we'd be truly dead." - Joss Whedon

690. "If there is no passion in your life, then have you really lived? Find your passion, whatever it may be. Become it, and let it become you and you will find great things happen FOR you, TO you and BECAUSE of you." - T. Alan Armstrong

691. "A strong passion for any object will ensure success, for the desire of the end will point out the means" - William Hazlitt

692. "There is no end. There is no beginning. There is only the passion of life." - Federico Fellini

693. "Rest in reason; move in passion" - Khalil Gibran

694. "Passion is the genesis of genius." - Anthony Robbins

695. "Our passions are the winds that propel our vessel. Our reason is the pilot that steers her. Without winds the vessel would not move and without a pilot she would be lost." - Proverb

696. "If passion drives you, let reason hold the reins." - Benjamin Franklin

697. "Chase down your passion like it's the last bus of the night." - Terri Guillemets

698. "Without passion man is a mere latent force and possibility, like the flint which awaits the shock of the iron before it can give forth its spark." – Amie

PATIENCE

699. "Genius is nothing but a great aptitude for patience." - George-Louis de Buffon

700. "Adopt the pace of nature: her secret is patience." - Ralph Waldo Emerson

701. "Patience and perseverance have a magical effect before which difficulties disappear and obstacles vanish." - John Quincy Adams

702. "Patience is the companion of wisdom." - St. Augustine

703. "Patience is also a form of action." - Auguste Rodin

704. "One moment of patience may ward off great disaster. One moment of impatience may ruin a whole life. " - Chinese Proverb

705. "Experience has taught me this, that we undo ourselves by impatience. Misfortunes have their life and their limits, their sickness and their health." - Michel de Montaigne

706. "Follow your heart, but be quiet for a while first. Ask questions, then feel the answer. Learn to trust your heart." - unknown

707. "Be patient toward all that is unsolved in your heart and try to love the questions themselves. Do not now seek the answers, which cannot be given you because you would not be able to live them. And the point is to live everything. Live the questions" - Rainer Maria Rilke

708. "All human wisdom is summed up in two words - wait and hope" - Alexandre Dumas Père

709. "The two most powerful warriors are patience and time." - Leo Nikolaevich Tolstoy

710. "He that can have Patience, can have what he will" - Benjamin Franklin

711. "The key to everything is patience. You get the chicken by hatching the egg, not by smashing it." - Arnold H. Glasgow

712. "Patience is passion tamed." - Lyman Abbott

713. "Patience serves as a protection against wrongs as clothes do against cold. For if you put on more clothes as the cold increases, it will have no power to hurt you. So in like manner you must grow in patience when you meet with great wrongs, and they" - Leonardo da Vinci

714. "Have patience with all things, but chiefly have patience with yourself." – St. Francis de Sales

715. "Patience is not passive; on the contrary, it is active; it is concentrated strength" - Edward G. Bulwer-Lytton

PERCEPTION

716. "Even a mistake may turn out to be the one thing necessary to a worthwhile achievement." - Henry Ford

717. "We can always choose to perceive things differently. You can focus on what's wrong in your life, or you can focus on what's right." - Marianne Williamson

718. "If the doors of perception were cleansed, everything would appear as it is - infinite" - William Blake

719. "It is one of the commonest of mistakes to consider that the limit of our power of perception is also the limit of all there is to perceive." - C. W. Leadbeater

720. "Blessed are they who see beautiful things in humble places where other people see nothing." - Camille Pissarro

721. "People only see what they are prepared to see." - Ralph Waldo Emerson

722. "There is nothing either good or bad, but thinking makes it so." - William Shakespeare

723. "If you look at your life one way, there is always cause for alarm." - Elizabeth Bowen

724. "What the caterpillar calls the end, the rest of the world calls a butterfly."   Lao-tzu

725. "Pain is a relatively objective, physical phenomenon; suffering is our psychological resistance to what happens. Events may create physical pain, but they do not in themselves create suffering. Resistance creates suffering. Stress happens when your mind resists what is...The only problem in your life is your mind's resistance to life as it unfolds." - Dan Millman

726. "Every exit is an entry somewhere." - Tom Stoppard

727. "The basic difference between an ordinary man and a warrior is that a warrior takes everything as a challenge, while an ordinary man takes everything as a blessing or a curse." - Carlos Castaneda

728. "The trick is in what one emphasizes. We either make ourselves miserable, or we make ourselves strong. The amount of work is the same." - Carlos Castaneda

729. "We cannot choose our external circumstances, but we can always choose how we respond to them." - Epictetus

730. "Man's mind, once stretched by a new idea, never regains its original dimensions." - Oliver Wendell Holmes

731. "The whole world is simply my story, projected back to me on the screen of my own perception. All of it." - Byron Katie

732. "As you inquire into issues and turn judgments around, you come to see that every perceived problem appearing "out there" is really nothing more than a misperception within your own thinking." - Byron Katie

733. "Could we change our attitude, we should not only see life differently, but life itself would come to be different. Life would undergo a change of appearance because we ourselves had undergone a change of attitude." - Katherine Mansfield

734. "If you are distressed by anything external, the pain is not due to the thing itself but to your own estimate of it; and this you have the power to revoke at any moment." - Marcus Aurelius

735. "When the only tool you have is a hammer, all problems begin to resemble nails." - Abraham Maslow

736. "Become a possibilitarian. No matter how dark things seem to be or actually are, raise your sights and see possibilities - always see them, for they're always there." - Norman Vincent Peale

737. "A stumbling block to the pessimist is a stepping-stone to the optimist." - Eleanor Roosevelt

738. "It's not what you look at that matters, it's what you see." - Henry David Thoreau

739. "We choose our joys and sorrows long before we experience them." - Kahlil Gibran

740. "A problem cannot be solved with the same consciousness that created it." - Albert Einstein

741. "Reality is merely an illusion, albeit a very persistent one." - Albert Einstein

742. "There are only two ways to live your life. One is as though nothing is a miracle. The other is as though everything is a miracle." - Albert Einstein

743. "We don't see things as they are. We see them as we are." - Anais Nin

744. "A man is as unhappy as he has convinced himself he is." - Seneca

745. "The place one's in, though, doesn't make any contribution to peace of mind: it's the spirit that makes everything agreeable to oneself." - Seneca

746. "Pain is inevitable. Suffering is optional." - Dalai Lama

747. "Nothing is a waste of time if you use the experience wisely." - Auguste Rodin

748. "A verse from the Veda says, 'What you see, you become.' In other words, just the experience of perceiving the world makes you what you are. This is a quite literal statement." - Deepak Chopra

749. "Whatever we focus on is bound to expand. Where we see the negative, we call forth more negative. And where we see the positive, we call forth more positive. Having loved and lost, I now love more passionately. Having won and lost, I now win more soberly. Having tasted the bitter, I now savor the sweet." - Marianne Williamson

750. "You must have absolute faith in your own perceptions of truth. Never act in haste or hurry; be deliberated in everything; wait until you know the true way." - Wallace D. Wattles

751. "Hurry is a manifestation of fear; he who fears not has plenty of time. If you at with perfect faith in your own perceptions of truth, you will never be too late or too early; and nothing will go wrong." - Wallace D. Wattles

PERSISTENCE & PERSEVERENCE

752. "Persistence is a unique mental strength; a strength that is essential to combat the fierce power of the repeated rejections and numerous other obstacles that sit in waiting and are all part of winning in a fast-moving, ever-changing world." - Bob Proctor

753. "You've got to develop mental strength. And you develop mental strength with the will. The will is the mental faculty that gives you the ability to hold one idea under the screen of your mind to the exclusion of all outside distractions." - Bob Proctor

754. "Fall seven times, stand up eight." - Japanese proverb

755. "Most people never run far enough on their first wind to find out if they've got a second. Give your dreams all you've got and you'll be amazed at the energy that comes out of you." - William James

756. "By perseverance the snail reached the ark." - Charles H. Spurgeon

757. "Perseverance is a great element of success. If you only knock long enough and loud enough at the gate, you are sure to wake up somebody." - Henry Wadsworth Longfellow

758. "Nothing is impossible; there are ways that lead to everything, and if we had sufficient will we should always have sufficient means. It is often merely for an excuse that we say things are impossible." - François de la Rochefoucauld

759. "Never, never, never give up!" - Winston Churchill

760. "Great works are performed not by strength but by perseverance." - Samuel Johnson

761. "A champion is someone who gets up, even when he can't." - Jack Dempsey

762. "Never Quit. "Don't ever, ever quit. Recognize that stopping now, regrouping to try a new approach isn't quitting. If you quit you'll regret it forever." - Rudy Ruettiger

763. "It's not whether you get knocked down; it's whether you get up." - Vince Lombardi

764. "Let me tell you the secret that has led me to my goal. My strength lies solely in my tenacity." - Louis Pasteur

765. "If you are going through hell, keep going." - Winston Churchill

766. "When you reach the end of your rope, tie a knot in it and hang on." - Thomas Jefferson

767. "I think and think for months and years. Ninety-nine times, the conclusion is false. The hundredth time I am right. " - Albert Einstein

768. "Success seems to be largely a matter of hanging on after others have let go." - William Feather

769. "Nothing in the world can take the place of persistence. Talent will not; nothing in the world is more common than unsuccessful men with talent. Genius will not; unrewarded genius is a proverb. Education will not; the world is full of educated derelicts. Persistence and determination alone are omnipotent." - Calvin Coolidge

770. "Character consists of what you do on the third and fourth tries." - James A. Michener

771. "Most of the important things in the world have been accomplished by people who have kept on trying when there seemed to be no hope at all." - Dale Carnegie

772. "The difference between perseverance and obstinacy is that one comes from a strong will, and the other from a strong won't." - Henry Ward Beecher

773. "The road to success is dotted with many tempting parking places." - unknown

774. "When the world says, "Give up," Hope whispers, "Try it one more time." - unknown

775. "Consider the postage stamp: its usefulness consists in the ability to stick to one thing till it gets there." - Josh Billings

776. "The greatest oak was once a little nut who held its ground." - unknown

777. "Fall seven times, stand up eight." - Japanese Proverb

778. "Perseverance is the hard work you do after you get tired of doing the hard work you already did." - Newt Gingrich

779. "If one dream should fall and break into a thousand pieces, never be afraid to pick one of those pieces up and begin again." - Flavia Weedn

780. "He conquers who endures." - Persius

781. "Stubbornly persist, and you will find that the limits of your stubbornness go well beyond the stubbornness of your limits." - Robert Brault

782. "I returned, and saw under the sun, that the race is not to the swift, nor the battle to the strong, neither yet bread to the wise, nor yet riches to men of understanding, nor yet favor to men of skill; but time and chance happeneth to them all." - Ecclesiastes 9:11

783. "The great majority of men are bundles of beginnings." - Ralph Waldo Emerson

784. "Keep on going, and the chances are that you will stumble on something, perhaps when you are least expecting it.   I never heard of anyone ever stumbling on something sitting down." - Charles F. Kettering

785. "Our greatest glory is not in never failing, but in rising up every time we fail." - Ralph Waldo Emerson

786. "Problems are not stop signs, they are guidelines." - Robert Schuller

787. "Vitality shows in not only the ability to persist but the ability to start over." - F. Scott Fitzgerald

788. "With ordinary talent and extraordinary perseverance, all things are attainable." - Thomas Foxwell Buxton

789. "Most people never run far enough on their first wind to find out they've got a second." - William James

790. "Difficult things take a long time, impossible things a little longer." - André A. Jackson

791. "Don't let the fear of the time it will take to accomplish something stand in the way of your doing it.   The time will pass anyway; we might just as well put that passing time to the best possible use." - Earl Nightingale

PROSPERITY

792. "The problem is that most people focus on their failures rather than their successes. But the truth is that most people have many more successes than failures." - Jack Canfield

793. "There are only two words that will always lead you to success. Those words are yes and no. Undoubtedly, you've mastered saying yes. So start practicing saying no. Your goals depend on it!" - Jack Canfield

794. "I have learned this at least by my experiment: that if one advances confidently in the direction of his dreams, and endeavors to live the life he has imagined, he will meet with success unexpected in common hours." - Henry David Thoreau

795. "Formulate and stamp indelibly on your mind a mental picture of yourself as succeeding. Hold this picture tenaciously. Never permit it to fade. Your mind will seek to develop the picture... Do not build up obstacles in your imagination." - Norman Vincent Peale

796. "There is no scarcity of opportunity to make a living at what you love; there's only a scarcity of resolve to make it happen." - Wayne Dyer

797. "Successful people form the habit of doing what failures don't like to do. They like the results they get by doing what they don't necessarily enjoy." - Earl Nightingale

798. "This is the law of prosperity. When apparent adversity comes, be not cast down by it, but make the best of it., and always look forward for better things, for conditions more prosperous." - Ralph Waldo Trine

799. "Any person who contributes to prosperity must prosper in turn." - Earl Nightingale

800. "The more tranquil a man becomes, the greater is his success, his influence, his power for good. Calmness of mind is one of the beautiful jewels of wisdom." - James Allen

801. "The greatest danger for most of us is not that our aim is too high and we miss it, but that it is too low and we reach it." - Michelangelo

802. "If you wait for opportunities to occur, you will be one of the crowd." - Edward de Bono

803. "Don't wait for extraordinary opportunities. Seize common occasions and make them great. Weak men wait for opportunities; strong men make them." - Orison Swett Marden

804. "True prosperity is the result of well-placed confidence in ourselves and our fellow man." - Benjamin Burt

805. "All prosperity begins in the mind and is dependent only on the full use of our creative imagination." - Ruth Ross

806. "Prosperity depends more on wanting what you have than having what you want." - Albert F. Geoffrey

RELATIONSHIPS

807. "Little kindness' and courtesies are so important. In relationships, the little things are the big things." - Stephen R. Covey

808. "The glory of friendship is not the outstretched hand, nor the kindly smile, nor the joy of companionship; it's the spiritual inspiration that comes to one when he discovers that someone else believes in him and is willing to trust him with his friend." - Ralph Waldo Emerson

809. "True friendship comes when the silence between two people is comfortable." - David Tyson Gentry

810. "I just do not hang around anybody that I don't want to be with. Period. For me, that's a blessing, and I can stay positive. I hang around people who are happy, who are growing, who want to learn, who don't mind saying sorry or thank you ... and [are] having a fun time." - John Assaraf

811. "A loving relationship is one in which the loved one is free to be himself -- to laugh with me, but never at me; to cry with me, but never because of me; to love life, to love himself, to love being loved. Such a relationship is based upon freedom and can never grow in a jealous heart." - Leo F. Buscaglia

812. "Shared joy is a double joy; shared sorrow is half a sorrow." - Swedish Proverb

813. "Remember, we all stumble, every one of us. That's why it's a comfort to go hand in hand." - Emily Kimbrough

814. "There's one sad truth in life I've found while journeying east and west - The only folks we really wound are those we love the best. We flatter those we scarcely know, We please the fleeting guest, And deal full many a thoughtless blow to those who love us best." - Ella Wheeler Wilcox

815. "If you were going to die soon and had only one phone call you could make, who would you call and what would you say? And why are you waiting?" - Stephen Levine

816. "Don't smother each other. No one can grow in the shade." - Leo Buscaglia

817. "Sometimes it is the person closest to us who must travel the furthest distance to be our friend." - Robert Brault

818. "Sticks and stones are hard on bones aimed with angry art, words can sting like anything but silence breaks the heart." - Phyllis McGinley

819. "You can kiss your family and friends good-bye and put miles between you, but at the same time you carry them with you in your heart, your mind, your stomach, because you do not just live in a world but a world lives in you." - Frederick Buechner

820. "Piglet sidled up to Pooh from behind. "Pooh!" he whispered. "Yes, Piglet?" "Nothing," said Piglet, taking Pooh's paw.   "I just wanted to be sure of you."" - A.A. Milne

821. "If fame were based on kindness instead of popularity, on understanding and not on worldwide attention, you would be the biggest celebrity on earth.   And to my heart, you already are." - Anonymous

822. "Lots of people want to ride with you in the limo, but what you want is someone who will take the bus with you when the limo breaks down." - Oprah Winfrey

823. "You cannot be lonely if you like the person you're alone with." - Wayne W. Dyer

RESPONSIBILITY

824. "Accept responsibility for your life. Know that it is you who will get you where you want to go, no one else." - Les Brown

825. "Promises are like crying babies in a theater, they should be carried out at once." - Norman Vincent Peale

826. "Everything you see happening is the consequence of that which you are." — Dr. David Hawkins

827. "Let everyone sweep in front of his own door, and the whole world will be clean." - Johann Wolfgang von Goethe

828. "Nobody ever did, or ever will, escape the consequences of his choices." - Alfred A. Montapert

829. "Simply put, you believe that things or people make you unhappy, but this is not accurate. You make yourself unhappy." - Wayne Dyer

830. "You must take personal responsibility. You cannot change the circumstances, the seasons, or the wind, but you can change yourself. That is something you have charge of." - Jim Rohn

831. "Freedom is the will to be responsible to ourselves" - Friedrich Nietzsche

832. "Responsibility is the price of greatness." - Winston Churchill

833. "Life is a gift, and it offers us the privilege, opportunity, and responsibility to give something back by becoming more" - Anthony Robbins

834. "If you want children to keep their feet on the ground, put some responsibility on their shoulders." - Abigail Van Buren

835. "The willingness to accept responsibility for one's own life is the source from which self-respect springs." - Joan Didion

836. "I try to live what I consider a "poetic existence." That means I take responsibility for the air I breathe and the space I take up. I try to be immediate, to be totally present for all my work." - Maya Angelou

837. "We are alone, with no excuses. That is the idea I shall try to convey when I say that man is condemned to be free. Condemned, because he did not create himself, yet, in other respects is free; because, once thrown into the world, he is responsible for everything he does." - Jean-Paul Sartre

838. "As human beings, we are endowed with freedom of choice, and we cannot shuffle off our responsibility upon the shoulders of God or nature. We must shoulder it ourselves. It is our responsibility."
- Arnold Toynbee

839. "Our duty is to preserve what the past has had to say for itself, and to say for ourselves what shall be true for the future" - John Ruskin

840. "Nothing strengthens the judgment and quickens the conscience like individual responsibility." - Elizabeth Cady Stanton

841. "If you mess up, 'fess up." - unknown

842. "Most of us can read the writing on the wall; we just assume it's addressed to someone else." - Ivern Ball

843. "When you blame others, you give up your power to change." - unknown

844. "Even when we know what is right, too often we fail to act.   More often we grab greedily for the day, letting tomorrow bring what it will, putting off the unpleasant and unpopular." - Bernard M. Baruch

845. "The best years of your life are the ones in which you decide your problems are your own. You do not blame them on your mother, the ecology, or the president. You realize that you control your own destiny." - Albert Ellis

846. "A new position of responsibility will usually show a man to be a far stronger creature than was supposed." - William James

847. "You are not responsible for the programming you picked up in childhood. However, as an adult, you are one hundred percent responsible for fixing it." - Ken Keyes, Jr.

848. "Few things help an individual more than to place responsibility upon him, and to let him know that you trust him." - Booker T. Washington

849. "Action springs not from thought, but from a readiness for responsibility." - Dietrich Bonhoeffer

850. "We are made wise not by the recollection of our past, but by the responsibility for our future." - George Bernard Shaw

THE LAW OF ATTRACTION

851. "As above, so below. As within, so without." - The Emerald Tablet

852. "Take the first step in faith. You don't have to see the whole staircase. Just take the first step." - Dr Martin Luther King Jr.

853. "You can have, do or be anything you want." - Joe Vitale

854. "I believe that you're great, that there's something magnificent about you. Regardless of what has happened to you in your life, regardless of how young or how old you think you might be, the moment you begin to think properly, this something that is within you, this power within you that's greater than the world, it will begin to emerge. It will take over your life. It will feed you, it will clothe you, it will guide you, protect you, direct you, sustain your very existence. If you let it! Now that is what I know, for sure" - Michael Beckwith

855. "Whatever we think about and thank about we bring about." - Dr John F Demartini

856. "Whether you think you can or think you can't, either way you are right" - Henry Ford

857. "Follow your bliss and the universe will open doors for you where there were only walls" - Joseph Campbell

858. "Man becomes what he thinks about" - Morris Goodman

859. "You know, when everybody starts to live from their heart, and go for what they want, they don't go for the same things. That's the beauty of this. We don't all want BMWs. We don't all want the same person. We don't all want the same experiences. We don't all want the same clothing. We don't all want ..... fill in the blank" - Joe Vitale

860. "Imagination is everything. It is the preview of life's coming attractions" - Albert Einstein

861. "You want to become aware of your thoughts, you want to choose your thoughts carefully and you want to have fun with this, because you are the masterpiece of your own life. You are the Michelangelo of your own life. The David that you are sculpting is you. And you do it with your thoughts" - Joe Vitale

862. "You can start with nothing. And out of nothing, and out of no way, a way will be made" - Michael Beckwith

863. "When you visualize, then you materialize. If you've been there in the mind you'll go there in the body" - Denis Waitley

864. "There's enough for everyone. If you believe it, if you can see it, if you act from it, it will show up for you. That's the truth" - Michael Beckwith

865. "We are unlimited beings. We have no ceiling. The capabilities and the talents and the gifts and the power that is within every single individual that is on this planet, is unlimited" - Michael Beckwith

866. "Our feelings are a feedback mechanism to us about whether we're on track or not, whether we're on course or off course. See it's the feeling that really creates the attraction not just the picture or the thought" - Jack Canfield

867. "We are here to change. We are here to grow, develop and unfold. We are progressive beings that have infinite capacity" - Michael Beckwith

868. "Learn to become still. And to take your attention away from what you don't want, and all the emotional charge around it, and place your attention on what you wish to experience" - Michael Beckwith

869. "All that we are is the result of what we have thought. If a man speaks or acts with an evil thought, pain follows him. If a man speaks or acts with a pure thought, happiness follows him, like a shadow that never leaves him" - Buddha

870. "You can begin to shape your own destiny by the attitude that you keep." - Michael Beckwith

871. "You give birth to that on which you fix your mind" - Antoine de Saint Exupery

872. "The greatest discovery of my generation is that human beings can alter their lives by altering their attitudes of mind" - William James

873. "Whatever you create in your life you must first create in your imagination" - Tycho Photiou

874. "Action will sometimes be required, but if you're really doing it in line with what the universe is trying to deliver, it's going to feel joyous, you're going to feel so alive, time will just stop, you could do it all day" - Bob Doyle

875. "See yourself living in abundance and you will attract it. It always works, it works every time with every person" - Bob Proctor

876. "As soon as you start to feel differently about what you already have, you will start to attract more of the good things, more of the things you can be grateful for." - Joe Vitale

877. "It's really important that you feel good. Because this feeling good is what goes out as a signal into the universe and starts to attract more of itself to you. So the more you can feel good, the more you will attract the things that help you feel good and that will keep bringing you up higher and higher" - Joe Vitale

878. "And you can break yourself free from your hereditary patterns, cultural codes, social beliefs; and prove once and for all that the power within you is greater than the power that's in the world" - Michael Beckwith

879. "Gratitude is absolutely the way to bring more into your life." - Marci Shimoff

880. "The best way to predict the future is to create it." - Peter F. Drucker

881. "The soul attracts that which it secretly harbors; that which it loves, and also that which it fears." - James Allen

882. "Your circumstances may be uncongenial, but they shall not remain so if you only perceive an ideal and strive to reach it. You cannot travel within and stand still without." - James Allen

883. "You are never given a wish without also being given the power to make it true. You may have to work at it, however." - Richard Bach

884. "Our subconscious minds have no sense of humor, play no jokes and cannot tell the difference between reality and an imagined thought or image. What we continually think about eventually will manifest in our lives." - Robert Collier

885. "Whatever you create in your life you must first create in your imagination." - Tycho Photiou

886. "You create your own universe as you go along." - Winston Churchill

887. "If you're thinking of debt, that's what you're going to attract." - Bob Proctor

888. "He is greatest whose strength carries up the most hearts by the attraction of his own." - Henry Ward Beecher

889. "Whatever you can do, or dream you can, begin it. Boldness has genius, power and magic in it. Begin it now." - Johann Wolfgang Von Goethe

890. "I am no longer cursed by poverty because I took possession of my own mind, and that mind has yielded me every material thing I want, and much more than I need. But this power of mind is a universal one, available to the humblest person as it is to the greatest." - Andrew Carnegie

891. "What lies behind us and what lies before us are tiny matters compared to what lies within us." - Ralph Waldo Emerson

892. "Follow your bliss and the Universe will open doors where there were walls." - Joseph Campbell

893. "What you resist persists." - Carl Jung

894. "Every intention sets energy into motion, whether you are conscious of it or not." - Gary Zukav

895. "What power this is I cannot say. All that I know is that it exists." - Alexander Graham Bell

896. "Your mind is a powerful magnet that will attract to you the things you identify yourself with. If you have sad thoughts, you will attract tragedies. If you are a good man, you will attract the company of good people." - Alfredo Karras

THOUGHTS

897. "Let a person radically alter his thoughts, and he will be astonished at the rapid transformation it will effect in the material conditions of his life." - James Allen

898. "You control your future, your destiny. What you think about comes about. By recording your dreams and goals on paper, you set in motion the process of becoming the person you most want to be. Put your future in good hands - your own." - Mark Victor Hansen

899. "Creation is always happening. Every time an individual has a thought, or a prolonged, chronic way of thinking, they're in the creation process. Something is going to manifest out of those thoughts" - Michael Beckwith

900. "Change your thoughts and you change your world." - Norman Vincent Peale

901. "The significant problems we face cannot be solved at the same level of thinking we were at when we created them." - Albert Einstein

902. "People become really quite remarkable when they start thinking that they can do things. When they believe in themselves they have the first secret of success." - Norman Vincent Peale

903. "You are a living magnet and you attract into your life the people and the circumstances that are in harmony with your dominant thoughts." - Brian Tracy

904. "Thoughts are sending out that magnetic signal that is drawing the parallel back to you" - Joe Vitale

905. "Your thoughts and your feelings create your life. It will always be that way. Guaranteed." - Lisa Nichols

906. "No problem can withstand the assault of sustained thinking." - Voltaire

907. "Whatever we think about and thank about we bring about." - John Demartini

908. "Our job as humans is to hold on to the thoughts of what we want, make it absolutely clear in our minds what we want, and from that we start to invoke one of the greatest laws in the Universe, and that's the law of attraction. You become what you think about most, but you also attract what you think about most." - John Assaraf

909. "As a man thinketh, so is he, and as a man chooseth, so is he." - Ralph Waldo Emerson

910. "I attract to my life whatever I give my Attention, Energy and Focus to. Whether wanted or unwanted." - Michael Losier

911. "A clear vision, backed by definite plans, gives you a tremendous feeling of confidence and personal power." - Brian Tracy

912. "What we think determines what happens to us, so if we want to change our lives, we need to stretch our minds." - Dr. Wayne Dyer

913. "Thoughts become things" - Mike Dooley

914. "Our life is what our thoughts make it." - Marcus Aurelius

915. "Change your thoughts, change your life." - James Allen

916. "Nurture your mind with great thoughts for you will never go higher than you think." - Benjamin Disraeli

917. "We are what we think. All that we are arises with our thoughts. With our thoughts we make our world." - Buddha

918. "By choosing your thoughts, and by selecting which emotional currents you will release and which you will reinforce, you determine the quality of your Light. You determine the effects that you will have upon others, and the nature of the experiences of your life." - Gary Zukav

919. "Thoughts are the shadows of our feelings - always darker, emptier and simpler." - Friedrich Nietzsche

920. "The ancestor of every action is a thought." - Ralph Waldo Emerson

921. "All intelligent thoughts have already been thought; what is necessary is only to try to think them again." - Johann Wolfgang von Goethe

922. "A man is what he thinks about all day long." - Ralph Waldo Emerson

923. "Always aim at complete harmony of thought and word and deed. Always aim at purifying your thoughts and everything will be well." - Mahatma Gandhi

924. "Thought is the sculptor who can create the person you want to be." - Henry David Thoreau

925. "Thought is the blossom; language the bud; action the fruit behind it" - Ralph Waldo Emerson

926. "You are today where your thoughts have brought you; you will be tomorrow where your thoughts take you." - James Allen

927. "Such as are your habitual thoughts, such also will be the character of your mind; for the soul is dyed by the thoughts" - Marcus Aurelius

928. "Man's greatness lies in his power of thought." - Blaise Pascal

929. "In my garden there is a large place for sentiment. My garden of flowers is also my garden of thoughts and dreams. The thoughts grow as freely as the flowers, and the dreams are as beautiful." - Abram L. Urban

930. "The revelation of thought takes men out of servitude into freedom." - Ralph Waldo Emerson

WEALTH

931. "Ordinary riches can be stolen, real riches cannot. In your soul are infinitely precious things that cannot be taken from you." - Oscar Wilde

932. "Wealth is the ability to fully experience life." - Henry David Thoreau

933. "Wealth is the product of man's capacity to think." - Ayn Rand

934. "Being rich is having money; being wealthy is having time" - Margaret Bonnano

935. "Only the man who does not need it, is fit to inherit wealth, the man who would make his fortune no matter where he started." - Ayn Rand

936. "If I were to wish for anything, I should not wish for wealth and power, but for the passionate sense of potential -- for the eye which, ever young and ardent, sees the possible. Pleasure disappoints; possibility never." - Soren Kierkegaard

937. "Early to bed, early to rise, makes a man healthy, wealthy and wise" - Benjamin Franklin

938. "Wealth is not a matter of intelligence it's a matter of inspiration." - Jim Rohn

939. "Wealth is not his that has it, but his that enjoys it." - Benjamin Franklin

940. "Wealth, like happiness, is never attained when sought after directly. It comes as a by-product of providing a useful service." - Henry Ford

941. "The question for each man to settle is not what he would do if he had means, time, influence, and educational advantages, but what he will do with the things he has." - Hamilton Wright Mabie

942. "It is not the creation of wealth that is wrong, but the love of money for its own sake." - Margaret Thatcher

943. "Don't judge men's wealth or godliness by their Sunday appearance." - Benjamin Franklin

944. "They say it is better to be poor and happy than rich and miserable, but how about a compromise like moderately rich and just moody?" - Princess Diana

945. "No man can tell whether he is rich or poor by turning to his ledger. It is the heart that makes a man rich. He is rich or poor according to what he is, not according to what he has." - Henry Ward Beecher

946. "The greatest wealth is to live content with little." - Plato

947. "for the majority of instances where money is desired for the admitted object of blessing others, the real underlying motive is a love of popularity, and a desire to pose as a philanthropist or reformer....If your real desire is to do good, there is no need to wait for money before you do it; you can do it now, this very moment, and just where you are." - James Allen

948. "They who are of the opinion that Money will do everything, may very well be suspected to do everything for Money." - George Savile

949. "The real measure of your wealth is how much you'd be worth if you lost all your money." - unknown

950. "I'd like to live as a poor man with lots of money." - Pablo Picasso

951. "It's good to have money and the things that money can buy, but it's good, too, to check up once in a while and make sure that you haven't lost the things that money can't buy." - George Horace Lorimer

952. "Money is neither my god nor my devil. It is a form of energy that tends to make us more of who we already are, whether it's greedy or loving." - Dan Millman

953. "Money is like manure.   You have to spread it around or it smells." - J. Paul Getty

954. "They deem me mad because I will not sell my days for gold; and I deem them mad because they think my days have a price." - Kahlil Gibran

955. "Money isn't the most important thing in life, but it's reasonably close to oxygen on the "gotta have it" scale." - Zig Ziglar

956. "The little money I have - that is my wealth, but the things I have for which I would not take money, that is my treasure." - Robert Brault

957. "It is neither wealth nor splendor; but tranquility and occupation which give you happiness." - Thomas Jefferson

958. "Wealth is not his that has it, but his that enjoys it." - Benjamin Franklin

959. "He is richest who is content with the least, for content is the wealth of nature." - Socrates

960. "Learning is the beginning of wealth. Learning is the beginning of health. Learning is the beginning of spirituality. Searching and learning is where the miracle process all begins." - Jim Rohn

961. "Whoever renders service to many puts himself in line for greatness - great wealth, great return, great satisfaction, great reputation, and great joy." - Jim Rohn

962. "Wealth is the product of man's capacity to think." - Ayn Rand

963. "All wealth is the product of labor." - John Locke

964. "If we command our wealth, we shall be rich and free; if our wealth commands us, we are poor indeed." - Edmund Burke

965. "All riches have their origin in mind. Wealth is in ideas - not money." - Robert Collier

966. "Money was never a big motivation for me, except as a way to keep score. The real excitement is playing the game." - Donald Trump

967. "Lack of money is the root of all evil." - George Bernard Shaw

WISDOM

968. "Knowing others is intelligence; knowing yourself is true wisdom. Mastering others is strength; mastering yourself is true power." - unknown

969. "Wise men speak because they have something to say; Fools because they have to say something." - Plato

970. "The well bred contradict other people. The wise contradict themselves." - Oscar Wilde

971. "Wisdom is not a product of schooling but of the lifelong attempt to acquire it" - Albert Einstein

972. "Never mistake knowledge for wisdom. One helps you make a living; the other helps you make a life." - Sandra Carey

973. "God, grant me the serenity to accept the things I cannot change, the courage to change the things I can, and the wisdom to know the difference." - Reinhold Niebuhr

974. "Sometimes I lie awake at night, and ask, 'Where have I gone wrong?' Then a voice says to me, 'This is going to take more than one night.'" - Charles M. Schulz

975. "A wise old owl sat on an oak; The more he saw the less he spoke; The less he spoke the more he heard; Why aren't we like that wise old bird?" - unknown

976. "The key to wisdom is knowing all the right questions." - John A. Simone, Sr.

977. "The highest form of wisdom is kindness" - The Talmud

978. "Wisdom is knowing what to do next, skill is knowing how to do it, and virtue is doing it." - David Starr Jordan

979. "A man only becomes wise when he begins to calculate the approximate depth of his ignorance." - Gian Carlo Menotti

980. "Wisdom ceases to be wisdom when it becomes too proud to weep, too grave to laugh, and too selfish to seek other than itself." - Kahlil Gibran

981. "The invariable mark of wisdom is to see the miraculous in the common." - Ralph Waldo Emerson

982. "I do not think much of a man who is not wiser today than he was yesterday." - Abraham Lincoln

983. "The next best thing to being wise oneself is to live in a circle of those who are" - C.S. Lewis

984. "Knowing others is wisdom, knowing yourself is enlightenment." - Lao Tzu

985. "Do not brood over your past mistakes and failures as this will only fill your mind with grief, regret and depression. Do not repeat them in the future." - Swami Sivananda

986. "The road of life twists and turns and no two directions are ever the same. Yet our lessons come from the journey, not the destination." - Don Williams, Jr.

987. "Live as if you were to die tomorrow. Learn as if you were to live forever." - Mahatma Gandhi

988. "By three methods we may learn wisdom: first, by reflection, which is noblest; second, by imitation, which is easiest; and third, by experience, which is the most bitter." - Confucius

989. "A wise man makes his own decisions, an ignorant man follows public opinion" - Chinese Proverbs

990. "A word to the wise ain't necessary; it's the stupid ones who need the advice." - Bill Cosby

991. "A man begins cutting his wisdom teeth the first time he bites off more than he can chew." - Herb Caen

992. "Honesty is the first chapter in the book of wisdom." - Thomas Jefferson

993. "The art of being wise is the art of knowing what to overlook." - William James

994. "The more sand that has escaped from the hourglass of our life, the clearer we should see through it." - Jean Paul

995. "The young man knows the rules, but the old man knows the exceptions." - Oliver Wendell Holmes

996. "To be satisfied with a little, is the greatest wisdom; and he that increaseth his riches, increaseth his cares; but a contented mind is a hidden treasure, and trouble findeth it not." - Akhenaton

997. "We are made wise not by the recollection of our past, but by the responsibility for our future." - George Bernard Shaw

998. "When I can look life in the eyes, grown calm and very coldly wise, life will have given me the truth, and taken in exchange - my youth." - Sara Teasdale

999. "Wisdom is found only in truth." - Johann Wolfgang von Goethe

1000. "Wisdom is not wisdom when it is derived from books alone." - Horace

1001. "Wisdom is the reward you get for a lifetime of listening when you'd have preferred to talk." - Doug Larson

Made in the USA
Charleston, SC
18 October 2016